Honey Does My Butt

Make These Pants

Look Big?

Swanhaven Manor
Elegant Retirement Community
300 Kennely Road

by Rebel Lowrey Covan

Swanhaven
Elegant Retire
300 l
S

Honey Does My Butt Make These Pants Look Big?

by Rebel Lowrey Covan

ISBN: 0-9702140-1-4

Original Artwork by:
Chelsea Covan

Printed in the United States of America
First Printing September 2002

Published by Dockside Publications, Inc.
Pensacola, FL
(850) 479-3305

ACKNOWLEDGMENTS

*W*riting a second book can be a pretty overwhelming undertaking, especially if one's first book was well-accepted. I'm tremendously grateful that mine was. Along those lines, I want to take this opportunity to thank all my wonderful readers (both known and unknown to me) who bought *I Know Why the Manatee Swims Naked (I've Shopped for Bathing Suits, Too)*. (And if you've bought this one, too — thanks again!)

This book would not have happened, nor would "Manatee," had I not been blessed by my loving and precious Heavenly Father with the gift of helping people laugh. For that, I am truly and forever grateful.

My one-in-a-kajillion husband, Les, has been a continuing source of strength, support, and encouragement for me — as well as once again being the most genial subject matter of so much of this book.

My beautiful, intelligent, funny daughters, Carly and Chelsea have — as always — graciously put up with being "used" by their "weird" (*their* word, not mine) Mom for "comic fodder." I truly believe I could never have been a humorist if I hadn't had them. They make *me* laugh every, single *doodah* day!

My much-cherished and beloved best friend/publisher, Lyn Zittel, has once again made a dream come true for me. She's long been my "biggest fan" and staunchest promoter. She's the hardest-working woman in the publishing "bidness" — and it shows!

My brilliant, fantastic, and extremely talented publicist, Judy Tashbook Safern, took a virtually unknown writer (that would be me) and introduced her to readers and bookstores throughout the South. More importantly, she's become a treasured friend.

Richard Williams, graphic designer extraordinaire, has again worked wonders with the masterpiece cover created by my extraordinarily talented *16-year-old* baby girl, Chelsea.

The hundreds *and thousands* of Red-Hatted women of impeccable style (and reading taste) that I've done readings for have made this "adventure" even more of "a hoot" than I could have ever anticipated. I thank them, from the bottom of my heart, for their support, and look forward to even more fun with them!

To Les, Carly, and Chelsea —
the loves of my life.

And, as always, to *"Bobo."*

Table of Contents

Ginny Balboa

After fighting valiantly these past five decades to survive the vast wasteland that *is* my mind, my memory — that last sliver left of the *advantages* of being "young" — has finally succumbed to that horribly loathsome four-letter word, T-I-M-E (or, as I refer to it, "The Totally-Indiscriminate-Memory-Eater").

What's strangest to me, though, is that I can tell you exactly what my Senior Prom date wore to that spring celebration in 1966 — right down to his saturation in British Sterling cologne — but I can't even *begin* to tell you what I had for lunch yesterday. From what I understand, however, this is the rule far more than the exception to it. As bizarre as it seems, many of my friends are experiencing the same "phenomenon." My husband refers to it as "selective memory" — the silly thing thinks *he* coined the phrase. I tried to tell him it's a term I've heard used many times to describe only the things one wants to remember. Sort of like his *hearing*. He has a theory about that. He has a theory about most things he does that I can't even begin to understand. For instance, with the "hearing" thing, I can recall that when we first started dating, he literally hung on my every word. Everything I said was fascinating, funny, deep, and well worth hearing. Even after we became engaged, he was able to not only hear, but *respond* to, the things I said to him. Then, we got married. Oh, the first two years were nothing to complain about — from a *husband-listening* standpoint. Then the conversations began to take on the following characteristics:

> Me: Honey, do you want to go see a movie tonight?
>
> Him: (from behind the newspaper) Sure.
>
> Me: What do you want to see?
>
> Him: Doesn't matter.
>
> Me: Something funny or serious?
>
> Him: I don't care.
>
> Me: How about something funny then?
>
> Him: Sounds good.

He goes to work, comes home and eats dinner. I get my purse.

> Him: Where are you going?
>
> Me: We're going to a movie.
>
> Him: Who are you going with?
>
> Me: You need to start taking off your wedding ring so you can hear what I'm saying.

His "wedding band" theory holds that after several years of marriage, a man's wedding band begins to cut off the flow of blood to his ears, rendering him, at least temporarily, totally and completely deaf — but only to his wife's voice. Oh, he can hear things like invitations from other men to go deep-sea fishing, and he can even hear pleas from his teenaged daughters for money to go to the mall; but his wife's words run together in some form of marriage-babble — sort of like:

Iwishyouwouldprunethosebushesinthefront yardtheneighborsarestartingtotalk,"

or something equally indecipherable.

His memory is great, though — for anything other than what *I've* said to him. Mine is a totally different story.

"Ginny Balboa," my Aunt Vestalee said to me at a recent family gathering after I had mentioned my failing memory.

"Ma'am?" I asked.

"Ginny Balboa. You need to get you some Ginny Balboa," she informed me.

"*Ginny Balboa?*" I asked her daughter, Vestavia, who was sitting nearby.

She simply shrugged. Aunt Vestalee has, over the years, created an entire language that needs its own dictionary. Once, she told me that Vestavia was having trouble in the "servy-cal" area, but that everything "come out fine wunst she had her pap smeared." She also told me that she was able to get the smoke smell out of her house after weekend visitors left by burning some "incest" left over from Vestavia's hippie days. So, you see why I had no idea who, or what, Ginny Balboa was.

"Don't be such a *maroon*," my aunt scolded. "It's to improve your *mammary!*"

Gingko (or *gengko*) biloba may be a wonderful way to improve one's memory, but it sure doesn't do much for one's vo-cab-lee-ary. That reminds me, I need to buy some more incest, get my pap smeared, and set an appointment for a . . . *mammygram.*

Move Over, Barbie!
Here Comes ... Maudine!

Barbie, that beloved and *"behated"* little size-two doll, finally has some competition. The Tonner Doll Company recently revealed its new "Emme" doll, created in the image of the plus-size supermodel host of E! Entertainment Television's "Fashion Emergency" program.

Emme (born Melissa Miller) is 5'11" tall, weighs 160 pounds, and wears a size 16. *Hallelujah!* It's only taken — what? — *40 years* for some doll designer to realize that there is no woman — *anywhere* (at least not on *this* planet) — that looks like a full-grown Barbie doll (although many attempt to do so). Barbie's simply not anatomically correct. I remember reading that if Barbie were life-size, she would measure something like 38-14-37. A 14" waist? *Please.* Even Scarlett O'Hara had an 18" waist. Most "real" women with the top and bottom of Barbie's life-size measurements have a waist somewhere near those sizes, as well.

While Robert Tonner, the Emme doll's designer, meant well, he appears to have fallen a little short. The newspaper photo of Tonner and Emme holding the doll shows yet another anatomically-incorrect representation. The doll doesn't even have underarm dingle-dangle, much less thunder thighs and a bulbous waistline. She just looks like Barbie's size-eight, elegant older sister.

Why can't they create *Maudine*, a size-16 redneck woman dressed in stirrup pants, a tank top, and white heels? Her additional wardrobe could consist of a muumuu; a two-piece, *way*-too-small bathing suit; skin-tight, stovepipe jeans; and platform flip-flops, *plus* a denim mini-skirt, tube top, and white patent-leather Dolly Parton-type high-heeled mules (the latter pieces to be reserved for weddin's and funerals). She'd have long, over-permed blonde hair with brownish-black roots. Her hair could be teased to infinite heights or put into a ponytail. She'd have long, purple acrylic nails with stars and moons imbedded into them — one nail should be missing, just for authenticity. She could carry a beer can, interchangeable with a lipstick-stained coffee mug that reads, "I got a bowling ball for my husband — good trade." Unlike Barbie's convertible and stretch limo, Maudine could come with a very old and rusty pickup truck with a personalized license plate on the back that reads "Big Mama" and an airbrushed, swirly one with rainbow colors for the front that reads "Bubba and Maudine." The truck would have to have a gun rack, nighttime hunting lights, eight-track tape player, car seat (not a child-restraint seat, but an *actual* car seat, preferably removed from the back of a Chevy Camaro, circa 1970) in the back for the kids, and a removable camper top because she and Bubba never know when "the mood" is gonna hit them while they're out driving around listening to Lynyrd Skynyrd. "'Free Bird' jes' makes Bubba a *wild man*," Maudine claims.

"Bubba" would have a "mullet" hairstyle (short on the top and sides and longer in the back — in Bubba's case, since his mullet is nearly waist-length — his is called the "Achy, Breaky, Big Mistakey," because of its close resemblance to Billy Ray Cyrus's former cut); and he would be skinny almost to the point of looking malnourished. He would come dressed in jeans (of course), with a thin, white undershirt — *not* a T-shirt, worn with an open, plaid, short-sleeved cowboy-type shirt with pearl snaps (no buttons for this man), cowboy boots, and a baseball cap with a dirty, stained bill from all those Chee-tos, pork rinds, and gallons of barbecue rib sauce. His extra clothes would be more jeans, more cowboy shirts, tank tops, camouflage huntin' clothes, huntin' boots, flip-flops, off-brand dirty tennis shoes with no laces, *and* a baby-blue polyester leisure suit, white socks and white patent-leather shoes (for the aforementioned weddin's and funerals).

Their young'uns, Destiny (the girl) and Chance (the boy), are just miniature replicas of their mom and dad, except that Destiny has a PermMullet. Chance has a mini Achy, Breaky, Big Mistakey because he's only five years old.

The possibilities are endless. There could be "Cousin Cooter"; "*Aint* Texie and Uncle Vester"; Bubba's best friend, "Booger Red"; and Maudine's best friend and hair permer, "Lacey Dee Turnipseed" (whose wardrobe can be shared with Maudine).

While these dolls may seem a little too "Southern" to most other regions of the country, the new line of "realistic" dolls can be modified to fit any locale — or even any other *country*, for that matter. This is just a start — and just a suggestion. But if given the choice of anorexic, bulimic, silicone-enhanced Barbie, the half-a-size-16 Emme, or the not-so-lovely, jiggly Maudine with the cottage cheese thighs, you can rest assured that Maudine's gonna be at the top of *my* next Christmas list!

A Very
"Uplifting" Experience

*W*hat *in the world is* <u>*this*</u>*?* I asked my daughters as I took a piece of unfamiliar lingerie out of the dryer the other day.

"What?" asked Carly

"This . . . this *bra-looking* thing," I responded.

"Oh, that's Amanda's Wonderbra," she informed me. "She left it when she spent the night Saturday."

"*Wonder*? As in 'I *wonder* why anyone would ever wear this bra'?" I asked.

"Oh, Mom. You know what those are," she told me.

"Well, yeah. I've heard of them; I'd just never actually *seen* one before. Where do your boobs go when you wear one of these things?" I asked, innocently.

"Up," came the response.

"Oh, so, even though she looks like she's a 36-C, she's actually . . . ."

"A 30-A," she answered.

Well, whatever floats their boats, I guess. Shoot, we didn't have anything even remotely like that when I was a 30-A. If you were a 30-A *then,* you *really were* a 30-A, and those "Susie Trainers" we had to wear offered no enhancements whatsoever.

I remember the humiliation I had to endure when my little nine-year-old sister, with revenge in mind for what she considered an earlier injustice, came strutting into the living room, wearing my first strapless bra around her head like aviator's goggles in front of a 16-year-old potential boyfriend I was trying to impress. It was a 28-AAAA.

Nowadays, though, I guess being flat-chested or "bustily-challenged" (to be politically correct) isn't a problem. Actually, though, come to think of it, it wasn't for everyone back then, either. We didn't have Wonderbras, of course; but that didn't stop Nan Anderson. She stuffed her bras with fresh white bread. What a great idea — *WonderBreadBras.*

The Class Reunion
Crash Diet

Mom! *What in the world are you doing?* exclaimed my daughter Chelsea, as she walked into the kitchen.

The island and the countertops were filled with nearly everything the pantry and refrigerator had once contained — everything, that is, that contained 500 calories or more.

"Look inside that envelope on the table. That should explain everything," I told her.

She read the piece of paper that had created my latest panic attack.

"Well, this is only an invitation to your class reunion. I don't get it."

"*ONLY* an invitation to my *class reunion*? *ONLY*? No, my darling, that is not *only* an invitation to my class reunion. That is an invitation to embarrassment, humiliation, and public ridicule! That's what that *really* is! Or did I not tell you that I weighed 98 pounds when I graduated from high school?"

"You did, Mom, but that was 35 years ago. Besides, you've been to class reunions since you graduated, and you weighed more than 98 pounds when you attended them," she attempted to reason with me. Bless her heart.

"Well, I haven't been to one since the 25th, and I was a whole lot skinnier then than I am now."

"Don't you think you're overreacting a little?" she asked me.

"*Overreacting*? I think *not*! I can see it all now. I'll walk to the entrance of the country club where they're holding this thing, and creepy, bird-legged Bill Matthews will yell, "Look, everybody, it's REBEL LOWREY! *ROLL* on in here, Rebel!' So, being the accommodating person I am, I'll lie down on my side, and your dad will give me a little push toward the food. Hopefully, it'll be downhill. Then, your dad and several of the other guys will help me back onto my feet, at which point I'll waddle the short distance to the buffet tables (after rolling over and squishing Bill Matthews), load four plates with whatever they're serving that's the most fattening, waddle to the table nearest the buffet, pull out two chairs and push them up against each other, after which I will sit in them, and proceed to eat. Three hours later, when I've finished eating, your dad and I will go out on the dance floor, where people will clear a wide path for me, as if they had a choice. Then, the singer will announce that they're having a dance contest, and I'll just *have* to enter. And guess what kind of dance they're going to be doing? The *Pony*, of course – the jumping-up-and-down-on-the-balls-of-your-feet, most unflattering and awkward dance that ever came out of the 60's; and let me tell you, honey, there were some bad ones. So, there I'll be, doing the Pony, while the seated onlookers are trying to keep their plates from shaking off the table, and the other dancers are ceding the victory to me — not because I'm so much better than they are, of course; but because they all want to be able to see their children and grandchildren again, without permanently wobbly eyeballs from having experienced 'Shaken Grandpa/Grandma Syndrome' any more than is absolutely necessary."

"Mom, do you realize how ridiculous you're being? You're not even fat," she tried to convince me. Bless her heart, again.

"Compared with Mama Cass and Orson Welles, maybe," was my reply. "But you know what — if I cut back on my calorie intake and start running, I'm pretty sure I can knock off this excess baggage before the reunion."

"But it says here that it's in six weeks."

"I'm talking about consuming no more than 100 calories and running 85 miles a day. Yeah! That's the ticket!" I was confident! I was optimistic! I was . . . *possessed.*

"Mom, you can't survive on 100 calories a day; and you know how winded you get just walking to the mailbox. How are you going to run even one mile a day?" she asked, sincerely.

"That's not the kind of support I'm looking for, you know, sweetie," I told her.

"I'm sorry. I really am. It's just that you're being totally unrealistic. You don't have to lose weight to go to that reunion. Besides, I'll bet you're not the only one in your graduating class who's gained weight," she attempted to console me.

"*Ah ha!* So you *agree* that I'm fat!"

"Not at all," she said. "You're *not* fat; you're just . . . ."

"If you say 'pleasingly plump', you won't see the outside of your bedroom 'til you're 45!" I warned her.

"I wasn't going to," she informed me. "It's just that you're blowing this whole thing totally out of proportion. I guarantee you, there will be a ton of people there who've gained a lot more weight than you have."

"Thanks for saying *'ton.'* I doubt that there will be; I guess I'll find out when I get there."

Surely enough, six weeks and six pounds later (I tend to eat more when I'm trying to lose weight), I showed up at my 35th class reunion on the arm of my 6-foot, 160-pound husband. Just as I had predicted, I was greeted by the now-hefty, and still-creepy, Bill Matthews. It turned out so much better than I could have ever anticipated. He was standing at the entry, eating off the buffet plate that rested — along with his mug of beer — on his wife's huge rear end.

Oh, and Les and I won the dance contest. It wasn't the "Pony," after all. It was "The Bump." Bill was disqualified for knocking Celia Cartwright into an amplifier.

I just *love* class reunions.

Do You Think June Cleaver Slept in Those Pearls?

I feel so sorry for young mothers nowadays. Harriet Nelson, Donna Stone, Margaret Anderson, and June Cleaver are all gone — except for those rare cable reruns. So whom do today's young moms emulate? "Married With Children's" mother-from-hell, Peg Bundy? Roseanne? Granted, and unfortunately, their households are certainly more representative of modern-day America than those TV families I grew up with — the Nelsons; the Stones (The Donna Reed Show); the Andersons ("Father Knows Best"); and, my personal favorite, the Cleavers ("Leave It To Beaver"). More's the pity. The only similarities I can find between the moms in these 50's sitcoms and Peg Bundy are, first, none of them worked outside their home; and second, they all wore high heels — *all the time*. The likenesses sadly ended there.

I'm at a total and complete loss to find *any* similarities at all between Roseanne and those 50's bastions of motherhood, other than that they were all married and had at least two children — and they all lived in two-story houses. Of course, they did all spend a lot of time in the kitchen — Harriet, Donna, Margaret, and June, cooking; Roseanne, eating. The four "Supermoms" apparently didn't eat many, if any, of the thousands of meals they prepared for their families. You simply cannot hide fat under those shirtwaist dresses they wore in every show; and not a one of them had any visible body fat. How totally unrealistic.

Then came "The Dick Van Dyke Show," with its bouncy Laura Petrie, and spelled "The End" for the shirtwaist dress, pearls, and heels. *(Yea!)* They were supplemented, if not supplanted, by Laura's flats and form-fitting Capri pants. I can only imagine how many women were grateful to her for that. Most men, too, were probably not at all opposed to seeing Laura in pants. My late Great-Uncle Dink was the exception. He complained, way back when "The Dick Van Dyke Show" first came on the air, and Laura "flaunted herself in front of the whole dang country in them skin-tight trousers" that the family, as we knew it, was headed downhill. His views on women who wore "trousers" were quite similar to those he held toward Hitler. They were both sent to destroy the world — one by genocide; the other by their subtle confiscation of the rightful male domain (i.e., "the world"). Well, I don't know about that, but I do know that if the women who watched "The Dick Van Dyke Show" were going to set about taking over the world, it would have been a heck of a lot easier to do it in Capris and flats than in crinolines, spike heels, and girdles.

And I think I've finally figured out why Harriet, Margaret, Donna, and June were always able to keep such immaculate houses. They never watched television — at least not in the daytime. That is *not* real life — except, perhaps, at my mother-in-law's house, which is also spotless. I, on the other hand, turn on the TV en route to the coffeepot every morning. Got to keep up with what's happening in my world and community, don't I? Then, there are all the food, beauty, and health tips on "Good Morning, America" — not to mention the timely tips on raising children. And one of these days, I feel fairly certain I'll be able to cook something that actually looks like the chocolate rose-petaled kiwi fruit crepe truffle compote that Martha Stewart showed me how to cook. The last time I tried it, it looked a lot more like banana custard sardine meatloaf — tasted like it, too. Then, of course, I have to watch "The Price is Right" so that I can be sure I won't be ripped off the next time I'm in the market for a $2,500 19" television. And I feel compelled to watch "The Young and the Restless" and "The Bold and the Beautiful" so that I can grasp just how good my life is in comparison to these neurotic, obscenely wealthy, devastatingly gorgeous, maladjusted people — lest I forget.

But, you know, it just isn't normal that they didn't watch TV in those 50's and early 60's idyllic sitcom households, particularly since television was so new and such a novelty back then. Shoot, at our house, when we finally did get a TV (in the latter part of the 20th century — *1958*), it was on from test pattern to National Anthem and flying jets.

And being so much under its spell, we all felt terribly sorry for poor, deprived Beav and Wally, David and Ricky, Jeff and Mary — and Bud, Princess and Kitten — no Mickey Mouse Club, no Howdy Doody or Captain Kangaroo. But, *boy*, were *their* houses clean!

Men in Cars

My husband and I recently returned home from a car trip. And we've both determined that we'll never again be in a vehicle together — unless someone else is driving. What is it that happens to a man when he gets behind the wheel of a car? It's like "Jekyll and Hyde." This normally. . . *normal* man turns totally into something else when he drives.

We all know the male stigma related to asking for directions. Has it ever gone any further than the following?

"Honey, don't you think we should stop and ask for directions?" I inquired.

"*WHAT* did you say?" he shrieked, his wild eyes rolling counterclockwise in his head.

"I mean, aren't we supposed to be heading toward Key West?" I asked.

"*And your point is?*" queried Dr. Jekyll.

"Well, we left Pensacola seven hours ago — and now we're surrounded by . . . mountains," I informed him. "There are no mountains in Florida."

"There are *now!*" he screeched.

"O-o-o-o-kay," I responded, beginning to realize that Tennessee can be a fun place to vacation, too.

Second scenario: "Honey," I implored, "don't you think we should turn on the windshield wipers? This is turning into quite a storm."

"Ah, this is barely a drizzle," he contradicted.

"Okay," I responded . . . as hailstones begin to chip the windshield.

And the following is one of my all-time favorites:

"Sweetie, the gas gauge is just above the little white 'empty' mark. Shouldn't we stop for gas soon?"

"Shoot, we can get to Brazil and back on what we've got in this tank."

Chug-chug-spit-spit.

Little Bunny Foo-Foo

I've decided that I'm not going to watch any more "Leave it to Beaver" reruns. They're too depressing. One I saw recently had June whining to Ward that she simply had to have "some help around the house" (i.e., a maid) because she just couldn't do it all by herself — the cooking and cleaning stuff, that is.

Well, in the first place, the woman, as my Great-Uncle Delroy referred to it, "never took a lick at a snake," i.e., *worked,* outside her home, so she had plenty of time to do all that housekeeping. Secondly, if one looks at the outside of the Cleaver home, one instantly realizes that this is, at the very least, a three-bedroom home, but more likely, it's a four; yet poor, ol' Wally, the perfect stereotype of the "red-headed stepchild" (although he was actually their biological son and had *brown* hair) had to share a room with the perpetually hygienically-challenged and creepy Beaver. Consequently, June had only the one bedroom of the boys' to clean, rather than two. Thirdly, I saw her cleaning one Saturday while wearing a kerchief on her head, tied Aunt Jemima-style, a shirtwaist dress with a crinoline ("stand-out") slip underneath, and, as always, those high heels and ridiculous pearls. I just wanted to yell, "June! Girl, go put on a pair of Wally's jeans, his football jersey and some Keds, for cryin' out loud! And stop dustin' the *bottoms* of those stupid vases! Nobody's *ever* gonna look there! And save those stilettos and those stupid pearls for a night out with your poor hen-pecked husband!"

I caught a quick glimpse of myself in the mirror a few weeks ago — on the day I did my annual housecleaning. Yesterday's mascara and eyeliner made me look like a raccoon. The University of Alabama sweatshirt that fit so well 20 years ago looked more like a long-sleeved tube top. My sweatpants fit like leggings. And to make the outfit even more chic, my bunny slippers had cocked eyes and only one ear. But I was a woman on a mission. I had kicked Les and the girls out of the house — to both their amazement and eternal gratitude, since I usually just make a cleaning list for them and leave them to it. For some reason, they never want me around on those particular days —among many others.

Then I set the stereo on an oldies station and cranked up the volume. Fortunately, the first song I heard was "Born to be Wild," so I dusted with a vengeance. It was followed immediately by "Light My Fire," so I was still on a cleaning roll. Then came "Born to Lose." It was so depressing, I had to lie down. A few commercials helped me regain my composure. Then, the worst thing possible happened. They played, "Do Wah Diddy Diddy." You know, "There she was, just a-walkin' down the street, singing 'Do Wah Diddy, Diddy Dum, Diddy Do, Snappin' her fingers an' shufflin' her feet, singin' 'Do Wah Diddy, Diddy Dum, Diddy Do,'" and it repeats those lines over and over and over again until they permeate and saturate what's left of your little brain and you sing it over and over again, no matter what's playing on the radio — or how hard you try to get it off your mind. It's like when your kids were little and learning all those songs in preschool, like "Little Bunny Foo-Foo" and "The Wheels on the Bus," and "The Itsy, Bitsy Spider," and they sat in their car seats in the back and sang them over and over and over, and you'd get to work after dropping them off and you'd be standing at the copier, singing, "Little Bunny Foo-Foo, hopping through the forest, picking up the field mice and popping them on their heads" while the people you worked with who didn't have kids looked at you like you were crazy. Well, that's how "Do Wah Diddy Diddy" affected me that day. I couldn't stop singing that annoying refrain — no matter what I did — and no matter what else I was listening to. So I decided the only way to get it off my mind was to sing something else. But all I could think of was "Little Bunny Foo-Foo," so that's what I sang, until I realized, to my total and absolute horror, that I was singing, "Little Bunny Foo-Foo, hopping through the forest, . . . *singing Do Wah Diddy, Diddy Dum, Diddy Do.*"

Ridin' the Storm Out

Hurricane season in the Southeast is something to be taken quite seriously. After having lived in the Southeast for the past . . . well, a *lot* of years, I've learned that being prepared is the key. However, regardless of the fact that I've spent my entire life in this part of the country, there is absolutely *nothing* to prepare me for being without electricity. And I've been without electricity for many, many days at a time due to hurricanes. I can live by candlelight . . . and I can also live on sardines, pork and beans, and bread, if I have to. But I simply *cannot* live without air conditioning. And to heck with the old saying, "Southern women don't sweat, they glow (or *glisten*, depending on what version you're hearing at the time)." Honey, I *sweat*! And I get really angry when I'm "glowing." It's like a never-ending hot flash. After three days without air conditioning, I once offered my firstborn child in exchange for my neighbor's compressor. My husband cancelled the transaction.

If hurricanes hit during the late fall or early winter, I could handle it. But June through the end of October? *Please!* Anyone who's spent any time in Florida knows that October *ain't* fall down here. October down here generally means we wear shoes with closed toes, but that's the only indication that summer's nearly over.

There's a lot of talk down here about "Hurricane Preparedness," i.e., the stuff you've *gotta do* and *are gonna need* if a hurricane comes to town. Under the "gotta-do" umbrella falls such stuff as bringing in your hanging baskets and pets for a Category 1 hurricane to bringing in your cars and your 400-year-old oak trees for a Category 5. We're told to stockpile things like drinking water, batteries, canned foods, first-aid supplies, candles, and kerosene lamps and oil. These personal supplies, however, are completely subjective and depend totally upon the individual doing the stockpiling. For instance, my Aunt Lou Ree's necessary hurricane supplies include Vienna sausages (A/K/A "Vyeener sawsidges"), Diet Dr. Pepper, and playing cards. My Aunt Raymie (Aunt Lou Ree's sister) has to have Krispy Kreme doughnuts, tomato juice, and more Krispy Kreme doughnuts. Aunt Raymie's baby boy, my cousin Luke, has to have his holey (and an embarrassment beyond compare to his momma) "I Love Hooters" (the restaurant) T-shirt. That's it — *just* the T-shirt.

The thing I understand least about hurricanes – or any other natural disaster — is the people who choose to "stick it out." Actually, that's the thing I understand *next to the least* about these things. What I actually understand the *very least* is how the news correspondents, whether CNN, the Weather Channel, or whichever, always manage to find these people and zero in on them for interviews, even though there are tons of those of us who have not only managed to graduate from high school, but college, as well. But we're never interviewed. *No way.* It's always "Bubba" who's hit on by the national media.

The following is a typical interview held between a

national news correspondent and the toothless ignoramus who has chosen to "ride out the storm." Here we go:

News Correspondent: "So, Mr. Numbskull, it appears that you and your family have chosen to ride out the storm in your mobile home here in the path of a 250-mile-per-hour hurricane. Would you care to comment?"

Mr. Numbskull: "Huh?"

News Correspondent: "I mean, do you want to tell us why you've decided to stay regardless of the fact that the entire area is under an immediate, mandatory evacuation?"

Mr. Numbskull: "Huh?"

News Correspondent: "Why are you still here in spite of this huge hurricane that's due to hit any time now?"

Mr. Numbskull: "Oh, this liddle ol' thang? Heck, this ain't nuthin'. Me and my brother, Bubba Two, was wunst holed up in a tree by a dadgum wart hawg for 17 hours up in Alabammer. This is jest a liddle ol' starm, ma'am. Me and my buddies ain't skaired o' no liddle ol' starm."

News Correspondent: "Well, Mr. Numbskull, the winds are predicted to reach well beyond 250 miles per hour. My crew and I are getting ready to evacuate. I'd strongly suggest that you and your 'buddies' come with us."

Mr. Numbskull: "Aw, no, ma'am. But thank ya a whole bunch. We got us some Jack Daniels, beef jerky, and sardines. We're all set. We ain't gonna let this spoil huntin' season for us."

News Correspondent: "Well, then, I guess we'll be talking with your survivors tomorrow."

Mr. Numbskull: "Huh?"

Swimming with the Dolphins — HA!

There are several websites on the Internet that are dedicated to encouraging people to "Come and swim with dolphins" — which is all well and good if you're seven years old or weigh 112 pounds. I'm a few years older than seven and a few pounds heavier than 112. Okay, *several* pounds heavier, so why would I subject myself to comparison with these lovely, sleek and slender mammals? How self-destructive is that to a chubby girl's already fragile ego? What I'm in search of is a "Swim With the Manatees" attraction. Although those wonderful creatures are much more graceful in the water than I — I swim like a cow that knows it's in imminent danger of drowning, and I tread water in much the same manner (arms and legs flailing like helicopter rotor blades in a desperate attempt to keep my head above water) — I *can* relate to what's going on in their minds. We're both thinking, "Yeah, just keep staring and whispering. I know you're talking about how fat I am and 'how could a soul let herself gain so much weight?' Do I look like I care? It's not as if I haven't *tried* to lose weight. I eat nothing but salads all day long — without dressing! It's not easy being fat, you know."

So, if I'm going to swim with any non-human mammal, it sure ain't gonna be a size-six dolphin. Nope. Just give me a herd of size-5X manatees and I'll be happy — until strangers start stuffing lettuce into my mouth. That's guaranteed to set the rotor blades in motion. Hopefully, they'll look closely enough to determine that I'm the one with the *small* nostrils.

The Evolution of Romance

Anyone who's been married for more than ten years and who's had a "relationship" leading up to that marriage can attest to the fact that romance evolves. I know. I dated my future husband for three years before we became engaged, and was engaged to him for three months before we married. Ah, those first few months. Dinner, dancing, movies, moonlight walks on the beach, extravagant gifts, "monthly-versaries" marked with flowers, hand-holding and gazing into one another's eyes. And there was no such thing as an argument — after all, he or she could do no wrong. And the goofy conversations:

Him: "I love you."
Her: "I love you more."
Him: "I love you most."
Or
Him: "*You* hang up first."
Her: "No, *you* hang up first."
Or
Him: "I love you, pookie-wookie."
Her: "I love you, my sweet little poodie-wacky-sacky."

Then you take the relationship to the next level — you get engaged.

At this level, you still go out, only not quite as often because that ring has to be paid for.

You start spending less time alone together and more time with your married friends.

Then you start actually planning the wedding.

His idea of the perfect wedding differs a little from *hers.*

He wants a wedding in her parents' living room with taped music. His best friend and her best friend will be their only attendants. There'll be a barbecue reception in the backyard. He'll wear a suit.

She wants a church wedding with 500 guests, a chamber orchestra, twelve bridesmaids and a sit-down dinner reception at the country club. He'll wear a tux.

They fight over this, she cries, and they compromise on a church wedding with 500 guests, twelve bridesmaids, a sit-down dinner reception at the country club, and he <u>will</u> be wearing a tux.

They make it through the wedding with their relationship and love basically in tact.

Then they go on their honeymoon. There's dinner, dancing, long walks in the moonlight, hand-holding, gazing into each other's eyes. And they relapse into the goofy talk.

"I love you, my big, strong, hubby-wubby."

"And I love you my beautiful, little wifey-for-lifey."

Then they come back from their honeymoon to the "real world" — long days at work, cooking, laundry, housecleaning, bills, and PMS — up close and personal.

Dinners are quite often like this:

"What is *this?*"

"What?"

"This *food.*"

"And what is *that* supposed to mean?"

"It just means what am I eating?"

"Well, what do you *think* it is?"

"I don't know. Soup?"

"Soup! You think this is *soup!* It's *meat loaf!*"

"Oh, I'm sorry. It's just that it's sort of . . . *floating*. It looks great, though. Really. Is this crepe for dessert, honey?"

"Crepe! *Crepe!* That's an *apple pie! Waaaaaah!*"

Then the baby comes, accompanied by exhaustion, post-partum depression, and the extra weight that won't go away — even after six months.

"I'm fat."

"Well, that's normal after a woman has a baby, honey."

"So you're saying I *am* fat!" (crying)

"*No!* No, I'm not saying that, I just . . . ."

"Well, you had a chance to say I wasn't when I said I was, and you didn't — so that means you think I am!" (more crying)

"No, sweetheart, I think you're beautiful."

"Even with my round face and pot belly?" (sniffling)

"Even with your round face and pot belly."

"*Waaaaaaah!* You *do* think I'm fat!" (crying full steam)

"Oh, *man* . . . ."

And as the years go by, and the kids keep coming — and *growing*, the only movies you see are rated "G"; the only hands you hold are your kids'; the moonlight walks on the beach are replaced by days on the beach spreading sunblock on little faces and constructing sandcastles. And dancing? Does the hokey-pokey count?

The gift-giving is not as extravagant — or as romantic — as it was in the dating stage.

"What's this?" she asks

"It's a Buttmaster."

"Did I *ask* you to get me a Buttmaster?"

"Well, no, I just . . . ."

"Do you think I have a big . . . *derriere?*"

"Well, no, I just heard you talking to Jen on the phone the other day, and you said your rear was getting too flabby, so I . . . ."

"Oh, good grief! Women *always* do that. One woman will say something like 'My thighs are getting *huge!*' and her friend will say, 'No, they're not, silly,' and the first woman will say, 'You really don't think so?' and her friend will say, 'You're my best friend. Would I lie to you?'

"Don't you do that with your male friends?" she asks.

"Men don't talk to each other about that kind of stuff."

"Well, you should. How else will you know when something's wrong with you?"

"We just let our wives tell us."

The Reality Fitness
Personality Quiz

Not too long ago, I came across a Fitness Personality Quiz that was intended to help those who took the time to take it — "Find the workout that will work for you." I must admit, I was intrigued. Here, finally, someone was making it simple for me to find just the right workout for my age, pounds, and (lack of) energy level. Yeah, well. Obviously, there ain't no such of a thing, because the options they gave me weren't realistic, by any stretch of the imagination. While it's a wonderful tool for those who actually *want to exercise*, I've added an extra option at the end of the ones provided (you should have no trouble identifying which one is mine). So, get out your pencil and take this fun, little quiz!

The thing I enjoy most about exercise is:
- o Enjoying the great outdoors
- o Surrounding myself with "fit" people
- o Feeling strong and dynamic
- o Melding my mind and body
- o Watching other people do it

The thing I like to come away from working out with is that I've:

- o Taken time to dig deeper into how my body works and feels
- o Brought mind and body together
- o Refreshed my spirit
- o Escaped
- o Earned the right to a huge margarita

I admire people who:

- o Are at the top of their game
- o Have reached their goals
- o Are comfortable with where they are in the world and with nature
- o Defeat the undefeatable
- o Can cause the manager of an all-you-can-eat restaurant to cry simply by walking through the front door

When faced with an overwhelming project deadline, I like to:

- o Give it my own personal spin
- o Draft players and make it a team effort
- o Go it alone — I don't need anyone's help
- o Deliberate over the precise line of attack for the project
- o Claim that the dog ate it

If my day has been horrific, I like to:

- o Contemplate over a cup of hot tea
- o Experiment with different relaxation techniques
- o Share my problems with those close to me
- o Spend the night watching a classic movie
- o Console myself with a gallon of Chunky Monkey ice cream

My main exercise goal in the future is to:

- o Feel tested and joyful
- o Become more gung ho
- o Get rid of those unnecessary and dangerous calories
- o Expand my suppleness and muscle tone
- o Not

I'd best be described as:

- o Mystical
- o Brave
- o Playful
- o Self-reliant
- o Chubby (but *very* cute)

If I'm going to exercise, it will be in:

- o Coordinated, expensive outfits
- o Sweatpants — nothing pretentious for me
- o Anything baggy
- o The latest hardcore clothes and equipment
- o Bed

Our lives should contain more:
- o   Achievement
- o   Amusement
- o   Stability
- o   Tranquility
- o   Spinach Dip

If I were to get lost in the woods, I would:
- o   Enjoy the serenity of the atmosphere
- o   Hike and pretend this was my home
- o   Panic and pray
- o   Be grateful for no intrusions or deadlines
- o   Wait for dwarfs to find me

Unfortunately, I didn't print the results of the quiz or what workouts are best for those who answered the "legitimate" choices. I *can* tell you, unequivocally, though, that if you selected all the final options, the best workout for you would be the soon-to-be-famous "TV Remote Control Workout." This is the one that will give you the strongest, most flexible *thumb* you could ever hope for. *Hey, it's a start.*

The Great Cupcake Caper

Standing in line at the grocery store the other day, another woman customer felt it necessary to explain to everyone else in line, and the cashier, the reason she was *buying* cupcakes for her kindergartener's class party.

"My firm had a huge deadline. Three of our attorneys were out of town at a trial. We were audited. The administrator had a nervous breakdown yesterday, and last night, my dog ate the TV remote control, my cat had fourteen kittens, and my in-laws moved in with us," she recounted in a most apologetic manner to all the strangers listening to her. "I've never sent my children to school with store-bought treats — *NEVER, NEVER!* I promise you all!"

The other moms gathered around her, sympathetically patting her on the shoulders. I just looked at her like the crazy woman I thought she was. What do kindergarteners care? They'll eat worms if they're chocolate-covered — and sometimes even if they aren't.

There are a lot of moms just like her, though. I even tried to be one. The first time was when some of the (other) moms in our subdivision decided to throw a big Valentine's Day party for all the children who lived there (and there were close to a hundred).

"Mrs. Covan, we'd like for you to bake the white cupcakes for the party. Mrs. Rockefeller is baking chocolate, and Mrs. Biltmore (I made up those names) is baking yellow," she informed me. "Oh, and I'll be sending you a list of all the names because you'll need to write each child's name on his or her own cupcake — just to make it all extra special for them."

"Of course," I responded, trying to figure out just where I'd find edible, nonpoisonous ink.

After calling several office supply stores and learning there is no such thing, I finally figured out that she meant that I should write the names with *icing*. Oh, well. No big deal. I'd seen it done at bakeries. All it took was a steady hand, artistic ability, and 43 years of experience. It's a shame 43 years of experience *eating* cupcakes don't count.

After coming up with what appeared to be the easiest and most delicious recipe, I set about baking — if that's what you want to call it.

Well, to begin with, for such little, bitty cakes, there was an enormous list of ingredients. Not only that, but it was snowing, and the roads were iced over, so I couldn't drive to the store. I knew I'd have to make do with whatever ingredients I had on hand. Anyone who has ever seen the inside of my pantry and/or refrigerator knows that's not very much. That was when I discovered that all flour isn't created equal. For instance, pancake mix *cannot* be substituted for all-purpose flour. And did you know that baking *powder* and baking *soda* are two entirely different things? Weird. That was the day I also discovered that one cannot use melted vanilla ice cream in place of vanilla extract. Who'd a thunk it?

And that was just for the cake part of the cupcakes. The frosting was a whole 'nother matter. For one thing, I would strongly suggest checking the expiration date on the milk bottle before actually using the milk. For another, adding baby powder to sugar *does not* make powdered sugar — not by *any* stretch of the imagination.

Another thing you might want to be sure you have on hand before you start baking cupcakes is *raw* eggs. All I had was the ones I had boiled for egg salad. I figured if I beat them with the mixer on high speed, they'd work. Not quite.

And food coloring. Now that's a piece of work in and of itself. I had used all mine last year for Easter eggs; but I'm thinking, "Valentine's Day — pink and red, right?" Red and white mixed together make pink. Ketchup is red; milk is white. Add a little sugar and *voila* — pink food coloring! The red was a little harder; but I found that if I used ketchup with just a little water and a whole lot of sugar, I could make the most delightful red. So I mixed those colors in with my frosting mix at just about the same time the cupcakes were to come out of the oven. I had always thought that cupcakes were supposed to be sort of "rounded" at the tops, like muffins. Maybe this was just a different kind of recipe. Mine were *sunken* — like little, tiny volcanoes. Oh, well, I could just fill them in with frosting and round them off at the tops. One teensy, weensy, little problem, though. I tried to get a couple of them out, but they seemed pretty permanently attached. That was okay; it would just make them easier to transport to the party. I'd let the Rockefellers and the Biltmores deal with them.

I kind of *applied* the frosting. Mostly, I just "ladled" it.

I'd never seen frosting actually "slosh" before. As for the rounding of the cupcakes, ... Well, *everybody* has round-top cupcakes. I was going for the volcanic look. It worked. And the writing of the names — *ha!* Have you ever tried to write "Elizabeth" on a *cupcake* . . . with a *turkey baster?* (I didn't have a frosting cone thingy. The baster was the closest I could come to it.)

Later that morning, I delivered the cupcakes (in the pans) to the party. You wouldn't believe the looks on the faces of the other moms. It was like they'd never seen muffin pans before!

"Who is 'Clog?'" asked Mrs. Rockefeller, as she attempted to read the names on my concave cupcakes.

"Oh, that's actually 'Clay,'" I informed her. "And 'Jiffypop' is 'Jeffrey.' You might want to give the one that looks like 'Phlegm' to Philip. 'Enema' is 'Emma.' Oh, and 'Hemorrhoid' goes to 'Anna.'

I had absolutely no idea what happened on that one. Doesn't matter. The moms wouldn't let their kids eat them, anyway. Come to think of it, I couldn't bring myself to let my kids "Crusty" (Chelsea) and "Catnip" (Carly) eat theirs, either.

The Price We Have to Pay for Eating Nanner Splits

There's a most unpleasant website on the Internet that's sponsored by MSN Health. It's called the "Dessert Wizard." Actually, I guess they intended for it to be helpful and a means by which we can all lose weight and attain better health. Yeah, well. I find it extremely depressing to learn that if I eat a nine-ounce banana split, I'll have to *mow my lawn* for approximately *two hours and 52 minutes* in order to burn off those calories. Even if I eat just a teeny, tiny, measly (two-ounce) banana split, I'd still have to walk for *one hour and two minutes* just to get rid of those few calories! If I eat a small (two-ounce) piece of cheesecake, I'll have to *run for 31 minutes*. (I'd be dead after seven, so that's not an option, anyway.) The only good news, for me, that comes out of this newfound, discouraging knowledge is that I *can* still have that nine-ounce banana split — only I'll have to *nap* for approximately *eight-and-a-half hours* to burn off the calories I've consumed.

So, will someone please turn off that overhead light and draw the drapes?

Thanks.

Purse Terror

One of the cutest things I've ever seen is the little 80-something husband walking around the mall, totally unashamedly, with his wife's purse looped over his arm while she shops or tries on clothes. Amazingly, they quite often match his little outfit. I guess, at a certain age, men just stop caring what other people think. Come to think of it, I suppose we all do, don't we? Well, by the time we're 80, I should hope we could.

Unfortunately, however, not all husbands are that uninhibited about their wife's purses. Many of them are much more comfortable with tarantulas. I mean, is it just *my* husband, or are there other husbands out there who suffer from "purse terror?" It's a certifiable condition — or at least it *should* be. A typical conversation evidencing "purse terror" follows:

"Honey, where are your keys?" he asks, naively enough. "I need to move your car."

"They're in my purse," I reply.

"WHAT? WHY? Why aren't they in the key basket?" he implores. "They're always supposed to be in the *key basket*!"

"Well, what's the big deal? I know where they are. It's not like they're lost or anything," I inform him.

"If they're in your purse, they *are* lost!"

"Don't be ridiculous," I chide him. "Just get them out of my purse."

"You've *got* to be kidding! I'm not going *in there*!" he notifies me, as if I've asked him to spend the night in "The House on Haunted Hill."

"Do you realize just how laughable you sound? Just get the keys out of my purse and stop being so silly."

"No *way*! *I'm* not going into that *thing*! I've been inside your purse before. Don't ask me to do that again," he splutters.

"Well, good grief. Just bring it to me, please. I'll get them for you."

He comes back in a matter of seconds, the strap of my purse held between his thumb and forefinger — and as far away from his body as his arms will stretch.

"Take it! Take it!" he pleads.

Thirty minutes later, the contents of my purse scattered in eleven huge piles on the living room floor, I've found the keys and thrown them to him in his "safe-viewing" position 20 feet away.

I simply cannot understand the man.

Practice Random Acts of Hunting for Garage Sales

America has become a nation of bumper stickers. It's getting harder and harder to find a car without one. Many attest to the driver's love for and allegiance to a particular college or university. Many declare that their children are very bright, while others claim that their kid many not be all that bright, but he or she can "beat up" the other driver's honor student. (And we wonder why kids nowadays are so violent.) Come to think about it, though, if *my* honor students get riled enough, they could probably take on pretty much anybody — not that they *would*, mind you, being young ladies "raised right" in the Deep, Deep South — but they most certainly *could*, if they had to.

Then there are the downright inhospitable stickers that more than likely make northerners feel less than welcome "down here," e.g., "We don't care *how* you do it *up north*." Those who are from north of the Mason-Dixon Line shouldn't take it personally, though. The people who display those bumper stickers probably don't care how "it's" done in the east or the west, either.

I have a cousin on my late daddy's side of the family who showed up at a family reunion a few years ago in a huge Cadillac with a bumper sticker that read, "Lose Weight Now, Ask Me How." Mattie Nelle topped the scale at . . . well, a whole lot of pounds, so *even I* didn't feel there was much need in asking *her* how.

Some bumper stickers express hostility. There's the very simple warning, "Forget the Smith & Wesson. This truck is protected by a pit bull with AIDS." (Well, as politically incorrect as that statement may be, a pit bull would certainly keep me away, so I guess the driver accomplished his purpose with his choice of bumper stickers.)

I saw one in Houston years ago that read, "Tailgate me and I'll flick a booger on your windshield." Charming. I stayed several car lengths behind him — even at red lights.

Then there are always the "Ask me about . . ." ones. There's "Ask me about my grandchildren," of course. But then, there are people like me who absolutely adore their dogs who have the "Ask me about my granddog." I know, "get a life."

Then there are the "Practice Random Acts of Kindness" displayed by people who were probably at the original Woodstock concert. Many of those are displayed next to "Legalize Marijuana" stickers. Flower people, I presume.

The ones that I find oddest, though, are the "I Brake For" stickers. There's "I Brake for Garage Sales," for one. I've nearly plowed into several of those because people searching for garage and yard sales are people possessed. You're driving down the road at 30 or 40 miles per hour when the car ahead of you suddenly *careens* across the road, driving much like Popeye Doyle did in "The French Connection" years ago, or they slam on their brakes. No turn signals, no warning, no nothing. Just brake lights, tires screeching, and a cowboy lamp with a Stetson shade is about to find a new home. And I'm on the verge of driving a rental car for several weeks while the body shop is scraping the taillights out of my radiator. And, you know, the irony of it all is that if I took those folks to court, they'd be able to get off by saying, "Well, she *saw* the bumper sticker."

It's the really off-the-wall "I Brake For" stickers, though, that keep me searching them out. There's "I Brake for Hallucinations" (more Woodstock attendees, obviously, so I'm gonna stay *way* far back from that one); there's "I Brake for Unicorns" (usually found directly adjacent to the one for hallucinations) and "I Brake for Manatees" (I feel pretty safe driving behind that one — unless, of course, they also have the hallucination sticker).

And the most politically incorrect of all: "The more I learn about women, the more I love my truck." Yeah? Well, you know what you can do with those dual exhausts — don't you, *Bubba?*

The one that I've never been able to forget, though, although I've tried very, very hard to, was one I saw in Atlanta in the late 80's. It was on a Matador with four different-colored doors. (I rest my case.) It read, "Is that your *face*, or did your *neck throw up?*"

Non-Kissing Cousins

Things have changed so drastically since I was in school — back during the days of the wooly mammoth and the saber-toothed tiger. I can still recall the horrible, scratchy old films narrated in that monotone drone that I had to sit through during P.E. on rainy days in "junior high school," a term found extremely funny by my teenaged daughters. One that really sticks out in my mind demonstrated to all of us sitting around in our one-piece, hideous, green gym suits how to "cry prettily." The film showed the "right" way and the "wrong" way young ladies should cry. The wrong way consisted of open-mouthed bawling and wiping one's eyes with the heel of one's hand or, heaven forbid, on one's sleeve. The "right" way, of course, required that our mouths not be open except to take little silent gasps of air, since our noses would probably be stuffy. And we were to always have with us, at the very least, a tissue; but much more preferable was a linen hankie. We were to use only the corners of the tissue or hankie to "dab" at our eyes "in a feminine fashion." We were never, *never* to blow our noses in front of people — no matter what, nor were we to "sniff," unless we could do so "delicately," without bringing attention to the fact that our noses were running like open hoses.

Yet another film demonstrated the proper distance to be kept between a young lady's body and that of her dancing partner. We were also taught how to giggle daintily with other young ladies if we were left sitting along the wall of the "dance venue," hence the term "*wall*flowers." This was to demonstrate to the young men along the other wall that we didn't really mind not dancing, and that we were "enchanting" and well worthy of being asked to dance. We were also educated in how to engage in light conversation with our dance partners. This repartee consisted of things such as the weather ("Hasn't the heat been dreadfully stifling lately?"), school ("Isn't it keen that our debate team is going to the finals?"), sports ("Didn't I hear that you're going to be the pitcher for our football team next year?") and music ("Don't you think Fabian's just *dreamy?*").

We twisted and ponied the night away at dances — well, until 9:00, that is. I remember the humiliation of having to go to my eighth-grade dance with my ninth-grade cousin. It's not that he wasn't cute or anything. As a matter of fact, I was the envy of most of the other girls there. It's just that he was, after all, my *cousin* — but he wasn't the cousin-marrying Jerry Lee Lewis kind of cousin, thank heaven. Of course, I'm sure it was even more mortifying for him to go with me — a skinny, little, newly-permed runt with a head that looked like it had a Brillo pad sitting on it — and not even those yellow, clip-on bows on either side of my kinky head could help it. My very popular cousin was the school's basketball star and was also very cute. That, however, couldn't cancel out the fact that he was my *first* cousin, and as such, had a family obligation that overrode everything else —

including the date he had for the dance with the school's very pretty head cheerleader.

I was at his house when the following conversation was held:

"Joan, sweetie," my mother beseeched her sister, "do you think Barry could take Rebel to the school dance next Saturday? I hate to even ask, but she's just transferred to this new school and she hasn't even met any boys yet, what with being in that ridiculous all-girl homeroom and all."

"Why, of course, hon. He'd be happy to," responded my aunt.

"I would *not!*" screamed my cousin from the den.

"Yes, you *would!*" retorted his mom.

"Awww, *man!*" was Barry's response.

So, my mom dropped us off at the school gym on the night of the dance.

"All right, Birdlegs," he informed me once my mom had driven off, "this is the deal. You'll walk at least ten steps behind me at all times. I *won't* dance with you, I won't *look at* you, I won't *talk* to you, and I *definitely* won't introduce you to any of my buddies. You got that?"

"My mom gave me $10.00 to give to you if you're extra-specially nice to me tonight," I told him.

"So, can you do the twist?" he asked as the dollar signs spun around in his eyes like a winning slot machine roll.

Actually, Mom gave me *two* tens to pay him, but I wasn't about to give the ol' toot-head twenty whole bucks just to be nice to me . . . birdlegs or not. I walked into the dance on his arm . . . with my little Brillo head held high.

Just How Tall WAS Your Hair, Momma?

My younger daughter, Chelsea, has been blessed with her daddy's thick, naturally-wavy hair. And it's more than halfway down her back. Consequently, in order for her to make it to school (less than three miles from home) by 7:30, it's imperative that she wake up two hours early to do her hair. If she chooses to wear it straight, it requires a good 30 minutes of drying, plus using the electric "straightener" on it. In order for it to be "wavy enough," that process requires gel or gunk and anything — absolutely *anything* — but hairspray. That's an abomination to the head of a teenaged girl. It can be tolerated for the prom, but that's definitely the only day of the year that it's allowed.

Heck, I used to go through three cans of Aqua Net a week when I was in high school. Had to keep that helmet head *smooooooth.* And that stuff could withstand a hurricane. There was no weather bad enough to make that hair flop when a girl used enough Aqua Net on it. Wind, rain, hailstones — *nothing* could bring down that "do." Nor could jumping jacks, trampolines, doing laps in 128° heat-index temperatures or even being thrown into a pool. Nothing at all could compete with that wonderful lifesaving hairspray. Those styles may have taken us two hours to prepare — what with all the teasing and smoothing — but they were there to stay. Proof of that was the four-plus hours it took to brush out all the hairspray and teasing.

I remember the hideous rumors (they were rampant everywhere) that spread throughout my high school my senior year about a girl at a rival school in town who had cockroaches set up residence in her beehive hairdo because she hadn't taken it down in months. Well, of course, her high school was saying that it was someone from our school who had the nest of cockroaches atop her head. Actually, of course, it was neither (unless it did just happen to be somebody from *their* school).

And I also recall that weird stuff, P-S-S-S-S-S-S-S-T that was supposed to save us girls when we were called for a last-minute date and didn't have time to shampoo. That was, of course, after the teased-hair era. One's hair had to be pretty much straight in order to use it, so I guess it was during and after "The Summer of Love" (1967) and at the time when Aqua Net's stock probably took a nosedive as girls (and guys) grew their hair as long as they could. Theoretically, I suppose it was a good idea. But in reality, it proved to be an absolutely nightmare for me.

I had received a phone call on a Friday afternoon from one of my best friends telling me that her gorgeous cousin was coming into town that night and wanted to take me out dancing — and would be there to pick me up in an hour-and-a-half. P-S-S-S-S-S-S-T to the rescue! And it worked wonderfully well. Actually, it worked until we got to the club where we were supposed to be dancing the night away. It wasn't until we got out on the dance floor — and under the psychedelic black lights that I discovered the downside of that new hair product. I was wearing a cute little black mini-dress and looked as if I'd just come in from a snowstorm. The "flakes" were covering my both my shoulders and my hair. I excused myself early, went home, and waited for my date to send me a bottle of Head & Shoulders shampoo.

Not having been blessed with the perfectly straight hair that was what everyone strived for in the latter part of the 60's, I had to resort to painful methods of straightening it (long, *long* before the days of the "electric straightener"). One technique was to sleep in orange juice cans — the *metal* ones. And for those of you who were smarter than I was, and opted not to torture yourself for the sake of vanity, the answer is "No, I didn't really sleep when I had those things in my hair." The other method was to bribe one's little sister to actually, literally *iron* one's hair. That entailed, as the term implies, that one actually place one's nearly waist-length hair on an ironing board while trusting one's little sister (who tended to have a really scary mean streak) to get the waves out of it without burning it off one's head. Sometimes, one's little money-grubbing sister even insisted on getting paid beforehand.

Nothing young women have to endure nowadays, hair-wise, can even compare with what we boomers had to go through. But they'd have it a whole lot easier — with the miracle-powers of my beloved "Helmet-in-a-Can" — *Aqua Net.*

Making Some
Really Big Changes

I s it just me . . . or does anyone else feel that he or she is the only person in his or her house capable of changing a roll of toilet paper? Or is it that we have no choice? My husband and daughters never take the blame for not changing the rolls. Their excuse? "I didn't use the last sheet." Of course not; they're far too smart for that. They leave anywhere from two to four sheets on the cardboard roll. They're right. They *didn't* use the last sheet.

What amazes me even more than that, though, is the fact that I find that I'm also responsible for changing the rolls in public restrooms, as well. Restaurants, libraries, airport terminals, department stores — *wherever.*

"Oh, just leave a couple of sheets on there," is the whisper heard from one stall to another. "Rebel's coming."

What a great claim to fame:

Rebel, the Toilet Paper Queen.

The Condensed Version of the All-Inclusive
Snowbird's Redneck Dickshunary

ABIDE: Tolerate ("I can't abide no sassy young-uns!")

AGGERFRET: Exasperate ("Them young'uns is about to aggerfret me to death.")

AIM: Intend ("I aim to marry her.")

AST: To question ("Ast 'em what they want for supper.")

AYGS: Something you can fry, scramble, bawl or porch.

BUB: Bulb ("The light bub is burnt out." OR "I planted some gladiola bubs.")

BUS: Bosom ("Her blouse was so low-cut, her bus was hangin' out.")

CELERY: Pay earned for doing a job ("He done so good, he got a celery increase.")

CHESS: Chest ("He's got so many chess hairs, he looks like a go-riller.")

CHESTER DRAWERS: Same thing as a chest of drawers.

DEVILMENT: Wickedness ("He's full of devilment.")

DROWNDED: To get rid of ("Alvis drownded his sorrows in Jack Daniels.")

DUHMATER: Tomato ("Them dang worms has rurnt all my duhmater plants!")

E-LEGAL: Against the law

EVER-WHICH-AWAYS: In all directions ("He was runnin' ever-which-aways.")

FAR: What burns in the farplace

FLUSTRATED: Baffled, bewildered, mystified, and confused

GEL: A site of brief imprisonment

GRAWN: Mature ("Little Betty Lou's all grawn up.")

HAY-ULL: The opposite of Heaven

HARD: Employed ("She was hard to be his new seckaterry.")

HE-ER: At this place

HICKEYDOO: Same thing as a doohickey, thing-a-ma-jig, or what-cha-ma-call-it

HISSY: Mad spell ("Mavis throwed herself a hissy fit.")

IDY: Thought ("She come up with a real good idy about the reunion.")

JAYBIRD: Bluejay ("Jaybirds is meaner than vultures ever even thought o' bein'.")

JIMMY-JAWED: To have a prominent lower jaw ("She'd be a right attractive woman if she wudn't so jimmy-jawed.")

JURY: A collection of jewels ("He bought her a rang at the jury store.")

KWAR: A group of singers ("Thelma Lou's at kwar practice.")

LEAST ONE: The smallest ("Dixie was the least one in the whole family.")

LESS: A contraction for "let us" ("Less go see a movie.")

LIDDLE OL': Small ("Skeeter was a liddle ol' young'un.")

LIKE: A deficiency ("He likes the drive to hold onto a job.")

LOCUSSES: Locusts ("They was set upon by locusses.")

LYEBERRY: A room or building where a collection of books, periodicals, etc. is kept. ("My lyeberry book is overdue.")

MASH: To press ("Mash on the gas pedal to get the car to go.")

MINT: Intended ("I mint to invite you.")

MISREMEMBER: Forget ("I misremember where I put my spectacles.")

NO 'COUNT: Worthless ("Bubba Junior is a no 'count, lying dawg.")

OKRY: Okra ("I like fried okry much better than fried green duhmaters.")

ONE: One or the other ("I told him to pick me or Wynelle, one.")

PARTIAL: A small, unwrapped bundle ("He sent it by partial post.")

PRIZE: To pry ("The door's stuck; you'll have to prize it open.")

RAISE SAND: Cause a commotion ("She raised sand when Marlow come in late.")

RANG: A piece of jury (see above) made primarily for the finger, but often found nowadays in/on many other body parts.

RENCH OUT: To wash by hand ("I have to rench out my nylons.")

RURNT: Ruined ("She rurnt my dress when she spilt grape juice on it.")

SALARY: Celery ("I like a lots of salary in my corn-bread dressin'.")

SECKATERRY: A typer

SINNER: Right smack-dab in the middle ("She always was the sinner of attention.')

SKINT: Scraped ("I skint my elbow.")

SNIKE: A long scaly reptile that crawls on the ground and is sometimes poisonous

SPELL: An undetermined period of time ("Come on in and set a spell.")

STUMP: To stub ("I stumped my toe.")

TAR: A hoop of rubber around the wheel of a vehicle ("He had a flat tar.")

TARD: Exhausted ("I am flat tard.')

TORECKLY: Directly, i.e., soon ("I'll be there toreckly.")

TOTE: To carry ("Junior, tote them gross'ries inside.")

THURPY: Treatment (can be physical thurpy, speech thurpy, occupational thurpy, etc.)

TUMPED: Turned+Dumped ("The canoe tumped over and nearly drownded Leroy and Hank.")

WANG: The part of a chicken made for eating, not flying.

Teen-speak

As a mother of teenaged daughters, I find myself having to master a "new" language every few months. I suppose every parent of teenagers throughout the ages has had to do the same thing. Back in "my day," we had "groovy," "far out," and, the very worst of all, "sock it to me."

Nowadays, though, it's not just the *words* kids use, it's *how* they actually talk.

For instance, I was sitting in a restaurant the other day in a booth adjacent to one occupied by what sounded like perhaps a 16-year-old girl carrying on a cell phone conversation. It went something like this:

"So, I knew I was gonna be like late, so I was like worried, and she was like, 'Don't be worried,' and I was like, 'I can't help it,' and she was like, 'You know, you like always do this,' and I'm like, 'I know.' Then she goes, 'Well, he won't be mad,' and I go, 'Yes, he will,' And she went, 'Well, he gets mad about everything,' and I went, 'Yeah, I know.'"

And *I* was like, "What in the world kind of language is *that*?!"

Adjectives also take on new meanings in "teen-speak." For example, "tight," in their vocabulary, doesn't refer to how last year's clothes now fit me. Instead, it's used, more often than not, to refer to a vehicle they're lusting after. And the hubcaps on those vehicles? Gone. They're "rims" now.

"Hard" doesn't describe what my stomach and rear end will never be again. It's a synonym for "good" — *I think.*

"Good," in teen-speak, isn't a synonym for "fine" or "high-quality" anymore, though. Now "bad" is good, as in "That movie was *bad*." But "good" *isn't* "bad."

I learned recently that I don't have a big behind. I now have what is referred to in "teen-speak" as a "ghetto booty" — although kids pronounce it "gheddo boody." It still sounds better than "big butt" — no matter *how* it's pronounced.

The Southern Baptist
Girdle Dance

Over the past couple of years, I've been asked to speak at a great many functions, ranging in size from a 10-person book club to 450 members of the Red Hat Society. These events are always tremendously fun for me and give me a chance to "pretend" I'm doing stand-up comedy again — although I call it "cheating" stand-up because, more often than not, I read from my book. That means, of course, *no memorizing!* At my age, that's very, very important.

One of the first things I'm asked by those who've never heard me read before is "Is your material clean?" Clean? Heck, I wish my *house* could be as clean as my "material."

Occasionally, I get calls requesting "references." Others just want to know what kind of groups I've "entertained." The most amusing one I've received thus far, though, came last week. A very nice, but timid, lady phoned me to say that she'd heard that I'm available to speak to groups. She then asked me what kinds of groups I've addressed. I explained that I'd done readings for, among many others, civic and professional groups, as well as "girls just wanting to have fun," like the Red Hatters. She then asked if I'd ever performed for church functions. I assured her that, yes, indeed, I had.

"What churches?" she inquired.

"Well, three have been Methodist; one was Catholic; two Presbyterian, three Episcopalian, and one nondenominational," I responded.

"Oh, . . . ," she said hesitantly, "well, I'll have to get back to you."

She called the next day and asked:

"Why haven't you spoken at any Baptist churches?"

"Well, the opportunity just hasn't arisen yet," I told her. "But, if it's any consolation, I'll be speaking at one next month."

"Oh, I see. Okay, I'll get back to you."

She called the next day.

"Our preacher said it'll be okay to have you speak," she informed me.

"And what denomination is your church?" I asked.

"Why, Baptist, of course," she responded.

Having been "born and raised" Southern Baptist, I guess I can understand her trepidation. Actually, I'm what my Great-Aunt Texie refers to as a "flip-floppin'" Baptist. I've been Baptist and Presbyterian, interchangeably, for the past 20 years or so. Besides the obvious differences in their dinners-on-the-grounds, the biggest distinction between the two is the fondness for girdles many older Southern Baptist women possess. I think that's why I switched "teams" when I was pregnant with my first child. It was absolute agony to have all those extra pounds resting on my bladder those last couple of months; but to have to go to the restroom during those few short minutes between Sunday School and Worship Service and see the prolonged and never-ending "Baptist Girdle Dance" going on beneath the stall doors while I'm dancing outside them in little circles. (Actually I'm pretty sure the Girdle Dance and the Waiting to Wee-Wee Dance are probably the only ones actually allowed in the *Southern* Baptist Church.) The contortionist moves of those girdled women would have been hilarious had I not been about to burst. The snapping, popping, grunting and grumbling coming out of those stalls were indescribable and incapable of being duplicated. My Aunt Luvenia was probably the worst. She managed to get her size 20 body into a size 14 dress every Sunday, thanks to the miracle of rubber; but everyone knew that if we didn't beat her to a stall, we'd never get into the one she was occupying. It was a full 15-minute battle with her girdle, accompanied by *"Dang! Dang! Dang!"* every single time she went to the bathroom. And she was still twisting, squirming, tugging, and, for all practical purposes, *dancing* — in full view of the entire congregation, all the way up the aisle to her usual seat on the second row.

Vanity, thy name is . . . *Luvenia ArkieDell Turnipseed Cheeseman.*

Out of the Mouths of Babes

O f the six buttons on my car radio, three are set on "oldies" stations, although I really don't care for that particular word. It's like "used" cars — which are now referred to as "previously-owned."

My children have been raised listening to "previously-heard" music. They can pretty much sing along with any Beatles song, even if they haven't heard it in ten years, because they were "gently bombarded" with this music from before birth until they were old enough to make their own music choices — quite often, especially of late, to their momma's chagrin.

Their exposure to "our" music (their father's and mine) came back to haunt us, though, when our firstborn, Carly, was three years old. I went to her *Southern Baptist* Sunday School class to pick her up after church service and . . . well, here's the conversation:

"Mrs. Covan, were you listening to an oldies station in the car before you got to church this morning?" asked Carly's young teacher.

"Why, yes, as a matter of fact, we were," I responded, amazed at her apparent psychic abilities. "But how could you possibly know that?"

"Because," she informed me, rather sheepishly, "Carly's been singing, at the top of her little lungs — for the past two hours — that Bob Dylan song, *'Everybody Must Get Stoned.'"*

We listened to classical music all the way home.

Thanksgiving Thighs
(And I'm <u>Not</u> Talking TURKEY)

*A*re you ready? my husband called to me.

"Ready for *what*?" I responded.

"Ready to go to the beach," he replied.

"The beach? The *beach!!* No! I am most certainly *not* ready to go to the beach. It's *January!*" I informed him.

"It is *not* January," he contradicted me. "It's *April*. And this is Florida. We always start going to the beach in April. You know that."

"Well, *I'm* not going. I don't care what month it is. I still have my *Christmas thighs!*"

"Your *what*?" he asked, rather dubiously.

"I haven't had enough time to work Thanksgiving and Christmas off my thighs. I *cannot* go to the beach yet."

"Well, honey," my husband addressed me. "If we're going to be perfectly honest here, those are the same thighs you had last year at this time."

"And whose fault is *that*?" I accused.

"*Mine?*" he asked, apprehensively.

"Well, I didn't get pregnant by myself, you know," I informed him.

"Our kids are *teenagers!*" he exclaimed. "How long are you going to blame your weight on *me*?"

"*Excuse me?*" I declared.

"I mean, it's been 17 years since our last child was born," he stammered.

"And your point *is?*"

"Nothing. Nothing at all. I think you look really good for your size, sweetie."

"My *WHAT?*"

"I mean your . . . your *age*," the poor thing responded.

"My *age?*"

"I mean you look good — *really, really* good honey," he replied, digging the hole deeper and deeper.

"Do you really mean that?"

"Of course, I do," he said. "Shoot, I've seen women *half* your age who are as fat as you. You're doing great."

What I'm trying to figure out is how this man has managed to be married to me for 22 years — and still have all his limbs intact.

And for the Main Course: Sherbet

Masochist that I am, I recently agreed to host a "small" dinner party for some long-time friends who are moving out of the country. It was blatantly obvious to me that there was absolutely no one else who could — or *would* — do it because *I* was asked to. These people (the invitees) have all eaten here, yet they still asked me to do it. That's overwhelming evidence that I was the proverbial "last resort."

I'm absolutely certain it wouldn't have been a big deal — for anyone else. There were only eight guests. No problem, right? And I chose a very basic menu — French onion soup, Caesar salad, roast beef and gravy, mashed potatoes, Brussels sprouts, rolls, and sherbet for dessert.

The "Rebel" version, though, turned out a little differently. I forgot to put the onions in the soup, so it was basically beef bouillon with bread floating around on the top. I put the salad in the freezer "for just a few minutes" because it had gotten a little limp while waiting to be served, and I wanted to "crisp it up a little bit," but I forgot to take it out until half-an-hour later. It froze, then sort of "melted." The roast beef was . . . well . . . charred, and the gravy was . . . well . . . the consistency of grout. The mashed potatoes sat too long in the water before I drained them, so they looked more like Elmer's School

Glue than any potatoes I'd ever seen. If there'd been anyone who wasn't too afraid to eat them, they'd have probably *tasted* like it, too. And the water cooked out of the Brussels sprouts pan, so they were sort of *blackened*, as were the rolls because I had set the oven on "broil" instead of "bake." Consequently, when I opened the oven door to take them out, the burst of heat instantaneously glued the mascara on my top and bottom lashes together.

As I listened to everyone drink their melted sherbet (the only edible item remaining), I sat there, comforted by the thought that this was my last dinner party — by *very popular demand.*

Betty Crocker is a FICTIONAL Character, Y'know!

I opened my front door recently to find my neighbor, Claire, standing there with a measuring cup in her hand. With good reason, I assumed she was sleepwalking, although it was 4:00 in the afternoon. Otherwise, why would she be at *my* house . . . with a *measuring cup?* (My reasoning unfolds below.)

"Hi, Rebel," she said. "I hate to be a pest, but I'm in the midst of baking cupcakes for Ashley's party at school; and I'm *so* ashamed to admit this, but I am totally out of baking powder. May I borrow some from you?"

"Baking powder?" I asked. "Now, what exactly *is* baking powder?"

"You are *so* funny!" she exclaimed. Then, after looking at the puzzled expression on my face, she said, "Oh, my gosh! You're *serious*, aren't you? You really *don't know* what baking powder is, do you?"

"Nope, not a clue," I assured her.

"Oh. Th-that's okay," she said, backing away from me as if waiting for my head to start spinning. "I-I-I'll go next d-d-door and get some from Lisa."

We've obviously never had Claire over for a meal.

Oddly, I found myself becoming somewhat jealous of Claire. Not only did she know what baking powder was – *and* how to use it, she was actually *baking* for her little girl's school party. My name was at the top (in *red* ink) of the "DO-NOT-Ask-This-Mom-to-Bring-Homemade-*Any-thing*-to-School-Parties" list after I brought homemade brownies to Carly's kindergarten Christmas party and little Ryan Roberts chipped his tooth on one — and they didn't even have *nuts* in them.

I felt I'd been given a second chance when we moved from Atlanta back to Pensacola, where no one knew about that little mishap. I had a chance to redeem myself when Carly's new first-grade class had their Christmas party. I decided to bake little individual pies. They were cute and safe, and, according to the recipe, relatively simple to make. I felt pretty good about the prospect of becoming one of the respected and beloved "Baking Moms" in my child's classroom.

I bought 24 of the tiny pie pans, and painstakingly followed the recipe directions in making the dough — from *scratch!* I even did the little "fluting" thing around the edges — tops *and* bottoms! I stuck them into the oven, and went to get dressed for the party, waiting for the timer to alert me that my teeny masterpieces were ready. I was *so* excited — until I took them out of the oven. They were a little flatter than I'd expected — and they didn't look anything like the picture in the recipe book. Well, thankfully, they weren't *black*, the normal color of my baking efforts.

I sprinkled a little powdered sugar (or something that *looked* like powdered sugar) on them so they'd look a little better. It didn't help much; but I had to be at the school in less than ten minutes, so I didn't even have time to go to the store to find something else to take.

When I arrived in the classroom, I placed my little pies on the table in the midst of all the "non-tooth-chipping" brownies and the beautiful, decorated cakes, cupcakes, and cookies. My pies looked pretty pitiful, but at least I'd brought something I'd baked myself. I still felt proud of my accomplishment — until the kids started eating them.

"Mommy, what *are* these?" I heard Katie O'Connor ask her mom (the baker of the brownies).

"I'm not sure, sweetie," Mrs. O'Connor replied, all the while examining Katie's pie suspiciously. "They look a little like tiny pies."

"But aren't pies supposed to have something *in* them?"

Well, that explained why they were so flat. That also marked the beginning of the pre-classroom-party notes my children always brought home with them, to-wit:

"Dear Mrs. Covan:

Mrs. (fill-in-the-blank's) class will be having a (fill-in-the-blank) party next Friday at 11:00. Will you please send or bring napkins, paper plates, plastic forks, or plastic cups for the party. Please don't feel obligated to bake anything. In fact, *please, please DO NOT bake anything*! We have that covered.

Sincerely, the Baking Moms"

Big Hips Sink Ships

There's been a huge ad in the newspaper lately for a "diet breakthrough" that promises to help its users lose copious amounts of weight in a very short time — something like 50 pounds in 40 days. The "before" photograph shows a very despondent young lady, slumped on a sofa, her eyes closed. (I guess her eyelids are too fat to open.) It's difficult to determine from this photo whether she's 50 pounds overweight or not overweight at all. (She's wearing *very* baggy clothes.) The "after" photo, on the other hand, shows (supposedly) the same young woman (a "model and TV personality") wearing an approximately size two, after-five dress, although she doesn't look a whole lot happier than in the "before" photo. (Personally, I think these folks need a new ad agency.)

I went online a few months ago when I learned that I'd be accompanying my firstborn baby girl on her "Graduation Trip" in June — a cruise to the Western Caribbean. My mission was to find "the right diet," i.e., one that would take 40 pounds off my body in eight weeks without my having to eat foods I abhor, give up the foods I adore, or do that foulest of all four-letter words: *exercise.* (Okay, it's an *eight*-letter word, but I had a point to make.) I'm still looking, and now it's approximately four weeks before the ship leaves port. The banana-and-peanut-butter diet I went on failed miserably, as did the fried-chicken-and-pecan-pie diet. Those were recommendations from a friend who claims she lost 100 pounds on the so-called "Two-Food Diet." She said that if you eat just the same two things three times a day for six months, the weight will just "fall off." What she *didn't* bother to tell me was that it was stuff like salads and fish or fruit and poultry that I was supposed to be eating. Like I'd just *know* what she was talking about. Do I *look* psychic?

Then there was the diet recommended by another friend. I was more than a little skeptical of this one, although she swore it worked for her. It entailed consuming fewer than 1,500 calories *a day* — not *an hour* — a *full day*— and exercising for *at least* 30 minutes — every single *doodah* day! Even *Sunday!* Yeah, like that one would work. Thanks, but no thanks. No more of those "combination" things for me— diet *and* exercise? Ha!

Susan, a longtime friend, called with her suggestion:

"Why don't you try one of those 'shake' diets?" she asked me.

"Honey, I shake every time I walk, and I *still* haven't lost any weight," I informed her.

"No, sillypants. I mean the *drink*," she clarified.

"You mean I can drink *shakes* and lose weight?" I was amazed.

"Of course," she responded.

"And . . . *no* exercise?" I asked, warily.

"Exercise would definitely speed things along, but you can still lose weight, even if you don't exercise. It'll just take longer."

"Well, make my reservations for Skinnytown because this is one diet I can stick to!"

I was excited! I was motivated! I was stupid. Two weeks, 42 shakes, and 10 extra pounds later, I realized she meant *diet* shakes. Was my face red— and was my butt *huge*! I should have known it was too good to be true.

Last week, out of sheer desperation, I gave in and went to a gym. I was desperate. I was frantic. I was chunky.

My husband suggested having my jaws wired shut, but I don't think he had *weight loss* in mind, if you know what I mean.

Another option was the gym. My experience with gyms has not been positive. Actually, it was traumatic and humiliating. Those were the worst 15 minutes of my entire life. It's a tribute to my strong will that I could even enter a gym again after what I'd been through. (My last gym experience including being on a treadmill next to a *jogging* 22-year-old, pony-tailed, 110-pound blonde, spandexed bimbo [with no bodyfat] named "Bambi.")

Chad, my personal trainer-in-waiting, showed me around the gym and introduced me to the "machines" I'd be using in my quest to find my hipbones. This was not fitness equipment; these were torture devices. There was one that had its victim sit with little padded thingies between her knees that were supposed to be squeezed together in order to (allegedly) firm her inner thighs. After that little demonstration, I realized just how sexy "flab" really is. Chad followed me out the door. I never knew I could run that fast.

I went directly — and very quickly — from the gym to the drugstore to buy some over-the-counter "appetite suppressants." Those are the last great hope for those of us who've tried everything else. Not necessarily a good idea, although I cleaned our entire house, washed all the cars in our neighborhood (boy, were my neighbors surprised when they discovered that), and waxed the garage floor — all in an amazing 47 minutes flat. Then I rewarded myself with a red velvet cake, which doesn't say a whole lot for the ol' appetite suppressants.

I'm not giving up, though. I've made an appointment with my doctor. She's going to prescribe those weight-loss patches for me. I *know* those are going to work. They can't fail. How could they? I'm gonna wear them over my mouth.

Aunt Dandie Pearl

My Aunt Dandie Pearl, the Fried Chicken Gizzard Queen of the Deep South, insists on driving, although she's well into her 80's and has to sit on three couch cushions to see over the dashboard of her 1972 pink Cadillac. She, like most octogenarians, has shrunken considerably since she bought her car brand-new 30 years ago. She went from *no* cushions in her 60's to *one* in her 70's, and now has three under her tiny, little hiney that enable her to see through that little space between her dashboard and the top of her steering wheel. The only thing one can see of her from behind her car is the very top of her little blue-haired head — and that's possible only because her car doesn't have headrests, and she has very *high* hair. She's cute, but she's really scary on the road. She doesn't speed, though. As a matter of fact, she's been stopped no less than 20 times over the past 10 years for driving *below* the minimum speed limit on the interstate. She's received both warning tickets and "real" tickets. After the first few, she claimed it was because she couldn't reach the accelerator, so her son, my cousin Parker, fixed that problem by adding a four-inch accelerator pedal extender thingie to her car. That didn't help, but at least she doesn't drive on the interstate anymore, for which all the Highway Patrolmen and State Troopers in America should be grateful.

She's hard to miss, though, on the highways and byways surrounding St. Petersburg, her home for the past ten years. Although she certainly blends in with the thousands of other little blue-haired ladies driving Cadillacs down there, there are a few subtle differences in their cars and hers. For one, she has a bouquet of plastic roses adorning her car antenna, a virtual menagerie of Beanie Babies lining the inside of her back window, and *live* Boston ferns hanging from either of her backseat clothes hooks.

She did get stopped recently by the local police, however, for "rolling through" an intersection clearly marked by a stop sign. The following conversation ensued.

"Ma'am, I need to see your license and registration, please," the polite and professional officer informed her.

"My *what* and my *what*, dear?" she asked him.

"Your driver's license and your car registration, please," he responded.

"Oh, my license is hooked onto the back end of the car, Officer," she told him. "Didn't you see it when you were behind me?"

"Ma'am?" he asked.

"It's hooked on just above the bumper. It has a big, ol' orange right smack-dab in the middle of it," she informed him.

"No, ma'am. That's your license *plate*. What I need is your *driver's* license. It's a little plastic card with your picture on it."

"Oh, dear. And where do you suppose that would be, Officer?" she asked him.

"Well, normally, it's kept in a person's wallet or billfold, ma'am."

"Oh, my goodness gracious me. I don't carry either of those things, dear. Anywhere else, do you suppose?"

"Maybe in your purse?"

"Oh, you mean my *pocketbook*?" she asked.

"Yes, ma'am, your pocketbook."

"But I don't carry a pocketbook, Officer. They're just too much trouble. But I do carry a sachet packet."

"Well, then, that's probably where it is."

"No, couldn't be there. All I keep in there is my lipstick and rouge."

"Ma'am, you *have* to have a driver's license to operate a vehicle," he told her, getting a little more exasperated, but still remaining polite.

"Well, I'm sure I do. Plastic, you said?"

"Yes, ma'am, plastic."

"Well, dear, I've been driving since I was eight years old. Drove my daddy's pickup truck in 1925, and didn't need any kind of license then. Doesn't experience count for anything? I've been driving for 77 years, you know."

"I'm sorry, ma'am, but you still have to have a driver's license," his patience starting to wear a little thin.

"Son, do you like fried chicken gizzards?" she asked, smiling her sweetest smile while reaching into the steaming Tupperware bowl on the front seat beside her.

Brown Leather, Knee-High, Designer Boot Camp

Those of us who have seniors in high school know that most mail nowadays isn't addressed to us— it's addressed to "The Senior" of the household (usually by name, so that those of us over 50 don't automatically assume we are the intended recipient). Since the beginning of summer, our senior (Carly) has received no fewer than 100 pieces of mail from colleges and universities all over the country. The latest was from some university in *Rhode Island* that had absolutely no idea how much money and time it was wasting sending its catalog to *my* child. It's a *good* day when I let her drive to the mall. Rhode Island? *Please.*

What's even funnier than those college and universities that have no clue is the different branches of the Armed Services that take the time and trouble to "woo" my firstborn child. All those seductive promises of world travel, funds for college, excitement, adventure, etc. won't faze her at all. Oh, she may be tempted by the "world travel" part, but only until she learns about the strings attached — like work — and discipline— and, heaven forbid, *uniforms.*

Attitude is a whole other thing. My husband and I tuned in one night to an episode of the survival game "Boot Camp." For those of you who missed it, the game consisted of contestants, i.e., *non*-military types, who were competing against each other, the elements, and the Drill Instructors (Marine, I think) to win a vast amount of money.

Carly walked through the family room as one of the "recruits" (contestants) was being verbally bombarded by her DI — actually, not just *verbally*, but *spittingly*, bombarded. He was so in-her-face that her eyes blinked with his every "p" word — "pitiful," "puny," "pathetic," — well, you know.

"I'd *never* let him talk that way to *me!*" Carly proclaimed.

"Oh?" I asked. "Not even for a half-million dollars?"

"Not even for a *whole*-million dollars," she announced.

"Well, what would you do if he got in *your* face?" I challenged her.

"I'd get right back in his," she responded, without hesitation.

"And end up confined to quarters for insubordination," I informed her.

"I'm *always* confined to quarters for insubordination, remember? That wouldn't bother me."

Knowing my child, I'm sure it wouldn't. It's not the possibility of the "in-your-face" screaming matches that would keep my future fashion-degree graduate out of the military, although that would certainly get her little fanny kicked out on the first day of basic training. Nope, it's the "outfits." I can imagine the scenario on her first day of boot camp as her Drill Instructor (or whoever has that scary task) explains the rules, regulations, and (worst of all) "dress code" — or whatever it is that they call it in the military.

"Ewwwwww! What are *these*?" Carly shrieks, her nose wrinkled with obvious distaste, disbelief, and disgust.

"Those, private (or recruit or whatever), are what you'll be wearing for the next (however many) weeks," her DI instructs her.

"Oh, I don't *think* so!" Carly responds, laughing.

"You *don't*?" asks her DI

"Good heavens, *no*! This color is *atrocious*! I look terrible in *any* color green, but especially in this hideous *olive*! And they're so baggy! No, thanks. I'll just stick with my own clothes. I brought some great American Eagle jeans; darling khakis; precious, little shorts; some really, really cute tops; and *tons* of shoes! Actually, slip-ons will look better with most of my stuff; but I can wear my Nikes for like tennis and that little obstacle thingie," she offers.

"Yeah, right," says her DI, laughing hysterically as she walks out the door.

The next morning — long before dawn — my daughter is awakened, quite loudly, by the same DI, the one with no fashion sense *what*soever.

"Will you *please* hold it down!" Carly mumbles sleepily from beneath her pillow. "Come back around 11:00, okay? I just got to sleep like an hour ago!"

Her DI doesn't seem to care. Carly is yanked, mattress and all, onto the floor.

"Get up, private *(or whatever)*! We're going on a lovely 20-mile hike in full gear at 0600!" her DI informs her and the rest of her "roomies," as Carly calls them.

"But it's gonna be like 120° *in the shade* today! Not only that, but I forgot my sunblock and SPF-35 lip-gloss! I cannot *possibly* go out in that sun without them! I'll look like *Clint Eastwood* by the time we get back!" she pleads, to no avail.

Ten minutes later, the DI comes back, only to find Carly dressed in a cute little pink Abercrombie & Fitch tank top and cotton running shorts, a matching A&F baseball hat, and platform, thong sandals. She's carrying her portable mini-fan (it's hot, remember?). Her hair is in a perky ponytail. Her makeup is flawless, considering how little time she's had to apply it. Her lipstick (although lacking sunblock) and eye shadow perfectly match her ensemble. She has her straw purse on her shoulder.

"That's like a really, really long way to walk, so I'm bringing my cell phone in case I get tired and need to call a taxi, or some of my friends need to reach me," she informs her DI, "Okay, I'm ready! Let's try to beat everybody else to the restaurant! I'm absolutely *craving* strawberry crepes! Oh, and will somebody please grab my CD player and that new Alicia Keys CD? Thanks! You're a doll! Remind me when we get back, and I'll give you a complete makeover!"

Well, you get the picture of why they're wasting their time. *Don't you?*

The Vast "Waist"land

Not too long ago, I made the mistake of glancing through a Victoria's Secret catalog. What a painful experience that was. Is it not an unfair world we live in where women not only overflow bra cups, but also have waistlines and no cellulite?

Granted, these models did at least have a little well-proportioned meat on their very long bones, unlike most runway models, but I long for lingerie catalogs for "real women" — like those Rubens painted — butt-nekkid, lying on their sides with a fried chicken leg in their hand. Those women were easily a size 16, but were obviously considered beautiful and seductive by at least one man.

The hardest thing for me about being overweight is that my faltering memory is good enough — unfortunately — to recall when I was thin — and I'm talking *really* thin here. I weighed 94 pounds when I got married — and that was long before eating disorders had even been diagnosed, not that I had one. I was just blessed with this "force" that I called "naturally thin." It's since been renamed "metabolism." Unfortunately, *meta*bolism has been replaced in my life by *mental*-tabolism, which has to do with the part of my brain that leads me to believe that there are more foods out there that taste really, really good than there are those that don't — included among the former are those chicken legs — unpainted by Rubens, but that I'm absolutely, positively sure were eaten by his models, even if they didn't make their way onto his paintings. You can't really believe they got those thighs by eating *spinach*, can you?

I'm actually very thin — from the chin up. It's just that the farther South (always, please, with a capital "S") one's eyes travel down my body, the less descriptive becomes the word "thin."

Case in point: The following is a conversation held a few weeks ago between my neighbor and me.

"Shouldn't you be wearing riding boots with those?" asked my neighbor and soon-to-be *former* friend, the size-six Rhonda, as I was unloading our family-of-four's weekly $500 worth of groceries from my car trunk.

"With *what*?" I asked, innocently enough.

"Why, with your *jodhpurs*, of course," she responded, as if I had any idea whatsoever what she was talking about.

"My *what*?" I asked, still totally unaware.

"Your English riding pants, silly — your jodhpurs," she informed me. "And just when did you start taking riding lessons?"

"These aren't riding pants, Rhonda. They're my khaki Capris. They've just considerately stretched to accommodate my thighs. As for horses, in case you haven't noticed lately, the legs these thighs are attached to are only about two feet long. A Shetland pony is pretty much the only 'horse' I could ride, and, from what I understand, they're not really *weight-bearing* animals. But thanks for pointing out my *'jodhpur'* thighs to me."

"Oh, don't mention it. Hey, do you want to come over for lunch? I made a huge Caesar salad."

"No, thanks. I feel a huge *fried chicken leg* coming on. I'm thinking of having my portrait painted next week."

Dating for Food

My good friend, Mary Elizabeth, has recently re-entered the world of Singledom. This is only her second venture into this world. Things are vastly different in Singledom now than they were when Mary Elizabeth first inhabited it. For one thing, in this, her most recent foray into Singledom, she now brings two surly, angst-ridden, smarty-pants teenagers, whereas her first companion was a wonderful 100+-pound Great Dane named Thor. This animal was a "dude" magnet extraordinaire. Mary Elizabeth would take him jogging with her in the many parks located in and around Atlanta in the early 70's, and would soon look like the Pied Piper, except that she was trailed by men rather than rats.

Dating in the 90's is a scary enough process for 20-somethings. I don't envy women Mary Elizabeth's age (she turns 47 again this year) at all. It was different in the "olden days," as my kids refer to anything pre-MTV.

In 1972, I slipped the "small-town" bonds of Mobile and moved to Atlanta. I was totally overwhelmed by the size and sophistication of that booming metropolis. I was also overwhelmed by the sheer number of single guys. I was most overwhelmed, however, by the abundance of department stores. Consequently, the greatest portion of my paycheck went to buy clothes and shoes, with just enough left over to pay rent. As a result, I was subsisting on oatmeal and grits, which was fine until I ran out of butter and sugar. That was when I started "dating for food."

Back in my shallower years (teens), I "dated for looks," i.e., the guy had to be really, really cute for me to go out with him. After that, during my "sensitive" years (the late 60's — the *19*60's, not *my* 60's), I realized just how shallow I had become, using how a guy looked to determine whether or not he was up to my expectations. It was during those sensitive years that I began "dating for cars" — Porsches, Corvettes, and the like. I was still in that mode when I moved to Atlanta, but it lasted only until I ran out of food. After two weeks of undoctored grits and oatmeal, I didn't care if the guy had three nostrils and drove a Gremlin. If he could afford to feed me, honey, he had a date for the evening.

It's still hard for me to admit that I actually did that. But I was *hungry!* The only way I can begin to justify it is to suggest that you picture feisty, little Scarlett O'Hara standing on that barren, dirt hill, clutching the dirty, puny carrot she had just pulled from the earth and taken a bite of — in her filthy, torn dress, with her nappy-looking hair. She held her fist up to the sky, and declared (with a mouthful of dirt), *"As God is my witness, I'm going to live through this; and when it's all over, I'll never be hungry again!* (Then there are some lines about "nor any of my folk," but *my* "folk" were all back in Mobile, eating fried pork chops, mashed potatoes and all that other stuff, while I was starving, so I saw no need to even mention them.) *If I have to lie, steal, cheat, or kill, I'll never be hungry again!"* Well, I wasn't *that* hungry; but I *was* determined to have a decent meal. At least I had gotten beyond using looks and cars as criteria for dates. Hunger is a fairly honorable reason for dating someone. It's not like I led them on. I provided them with intelligent, sometimes witty, conversation (between bites) in exchange for meat, fish, poultry or whatever. It was purely for survival. Besides, they had to eat, too.

There were certain drawbacks to this particular type of dating. While looks and vehicles did not enter into this particular dating process for me, I still ended up with some pretty repulsive dates. Among the worst was one Woody-Allenesque creep who asked me if I'd like a demonstration of his ability to pull his bottom lip over his head.

I didn't.

Well, fortunately for Mary Elizabeth, she's mature enough to not care about how a guy looks; she drives a Lexus; and she can pay for her own food. She just doesn't know how or where to meet good men. I found it rather funny that she came to me for advice. Actually, I found it quite hilarious. I've been married for more than 20 years. Things have changed a bit since I last dated. *Men* have changed quite a bit since I last dated. Heck, for that matter, *dirt* has changed a bit since *I* last dated. I did, however, warn her against looking in bars, although that was pretty socially acceptable in the "olden days." By way of example, I recounted to her the time, in 1988, when I went to a friend's bachelorette party at a club in Atlanta that catered to baby-boomers, and specialized in 50's and 60's music. There were about 20 of us attendees (all women, of course) gathered there. Being happily married, as were most of the other women in my group, I was certainly not "looking." I was more into "avoid" mode. Yet, as I sat there talking with several of my friends, a rather obnoxious guy "slouched" up to me. He looked sort of like Elvis. Actually, he looked like Elvis *would have* looked — if he had had eleven more years to eat.

"Y'wanna *daince*?" he slurred.

I didn't.

"Y'*shore*?" he asked.

I was.

So, fearing fat Elvis look-a-likes and men with floor-dragging lower lips, Mary Elizabeth has decided to forego dating for a while.

Smart girl.

Dinner on the Grounds

There's a little funny that's been making the rounds on the Internet lately. It's entitled "Southern Girls," and it consists of some of the delightful characteristics of us "Southern girls." One of the facts it points out is that Southern girls "have a distinct way with fond expressions," e.g., "Y'all come back," "Well, bless your heart," "How's your mother," and "Love your hair," (whether we do or not). Another is that Southern girls know everybody's first name: Honey, Darlin', and Sugah. We know the movies that speak to our hearts: "Gone With the Wind," "Fried Green Tomatoes," "Driving Miss Daisy," and "Steel Magnolias." Since this list came out before the movie, I have to add (in my own opinion, of course) that "Divine Secrets of the Ya-Ya Sisterhood" must now be included.

The list goes on to state that Southern girls also know their elegant gentlemen: "Men in uniform, men in tuxedoes, and Rhett Butler, of course."

My personal favorite, though, is that Southern girls know their religions: Baptist, Methodist and Football (I might add the further clarification that most Southern girls' favorite football "religion" would definitely be the Southeastern Conference, and I'll argue that one to my grave, *"Sugah!"*).

I was, as we say down here, "born and raised Southern Baptist," although I've kinda gone back and forth from

Southern Baptist to Presbyterian over the past several years. There's not that much difference, I can assure you. As someone once said, a Presbyterian (also known as "God's frozen chosen") is just a Southern Baptist with a college education. But I know lots and lots of Southern Baptists with college degrees, and they'd probably never convert.

The biggest difference I've found in the Southern Baptist and Presbyterian churches I've attended is "dinner on the grounds." The first time I heard that expression, many, many, *many* years ago, when I was a wee child, I visualized all the food being spread out on the ant-covered grass — I still think they could come up with a better name for it, like dinner *on the tables* on the grounds.

But, oh, those Southern Baptist dinners on the grounds of my youth — fried chicken, butterbeans and peas, fried okra, creamed corn, corn pudding, turnip greens and collard greens, cornbread, biscuits, and tables full of desserts, plus iced tea so sweet it should've been on the dessert table. Those are the foods of my childhood and the foods I grew up on. They were served, for many years, in our mother's and grandmother's best Blue Willow china, Fiestaware, or Depression glass — until Tupperware was invented. They were served with pride and with uncontained eagerness to see that whatever dishes they had brought were returned home empty. It was the only acceptable condition. Same thing at family reunions. We had such a huge, extended family — great-aunts and great-uncles and first, second and third cousins — that I never knew half the people there; but that was okay, I was only there to make my Mamaw happy and, of course, for the food — and, boy oh boy, was it wonderful! Well, it was wonderful until Colonel Sanders came onto the scene, that is. It was an abomination to my eyes — of the very worst kind — the first time I went to a family reunion and saw that red-and-white striped bucket sitting on it. There might as well have been a pink-furred monkey in leotards sitting on that table. That's how out of place that bucket looked. It had been brought by my Aunt Vonzelle's daughter-in-law (from *Canada*, I might add). She had only been in the family for two months. We forgave her because she just didn't know any better — she was not only *not* a Southerner, she wasn't even from the United States. Well, little did we know what a horrible influence she was going to have on the rest of our family ("the lazy ones," as my aunts came to refer to them). Sure enough, the very next year, lo and behold, that table was filled with boxes and buckets of "store-bought" chicken; but even worse were the offensive store-bought pies and cakes and, worst of all, a *pizza box!* Well, when we saw that, we all knew that my great-granny was spinning in her grave. (Not a great visual, I can assure you.)

Not wanting to be a hypocrite, and trying to comply with my Mamaw's sincere request that all her grand-children (and great-grandchildren) be as honest and truthful as we can possibly be, I must admit that I, too, have backslidden — more than once. Anyone who's ever read anything about my (lack of) cooking skills knows that even if I did bother to cook, no one would eat it if they knew I'd prepared it. Consequently, I fell into that old trap of buying store-bought and restaurant-cooked food for the reunions. Only I was smarter than most – at least *I* put *mine* into a Tupperware dish, making it look as if I'd slaved over it for hours. There are still those who think I must have resorted to using Super Glue to finally get the crust on my fried chicken to actually adhere to the meat. Only I — *and Colonel Sanders* — know for sure.

I Don't Want An <u>Empty</u> Nest, Just A <u>Clean</u> One

Rebel! Get over here quick! We're having a party! my friend Lesley cheerfully informed me over the phone.

"What's the occasion?" I asked.

"The twins just left for college, and I'm celebrating big-time!" she responded in the most jubilant tone of voice I've ever heard her use.

"But why are you celebrating? I thought you said they just left for college."

"Well, *goofy*, what better reason to celebrate?" she inquired. "I have my house back, I have my phone back, I have my car back, I have my clothes back! I have my *life* back! So, get on over here now! Judi and Kathy are already here. Diane and Brenda are on their way. I'm fixin' to call Sara and Vicky now. So, hurry up and get over here!"

"Okay, I'll be there in just a little bit," I told her.

After I hung up the phone, I sat there still trying to determine why she was so rejoiceful. Lesley's twin girls were her only children, yet she seemed genuinely happy that they were heading off to college in a town nearly 1,000 miles away.

I've been hiding all the college brochures that have been coming in the mail for Carly, our firstborn. She's a junior in high school now, so I guess it's expected that we'd be deluged with them. I'm just not ready to think about that yet. (Scarlett O'Hara and I have the same hang-up.)

I've talked with many of the moms of Carly's friends who have the same mindset as Lesley — empty that nest as quickly as possible. Not me. I don't want an *empty* nest, just a *clean* one. I don't want my little birdies to fly. It seems as if they just "hatched."

What I have in mind is one of those "Southfork" scenarios. You know, the huge house with enough room for the girls, their husbands, and all our grand . . . , our grandch . . . — our childrens' kids.

"Forget about it, Mom," Carly interrupted my daydreaming. "That'll never happen."

"But why not? It worked for the Ewings on 'Dallas.' You wouldn't have a mortgage payment. You wouldn't have grocery or utility bills. You wouldn't have . . . ."

"A *life*," Chelsea interjected.

"That's not fair," I commented.

"I can just picture it now," Chelsea said. "We're living with you and Dad at Southspoon, ..."

"South*fork*," I corrected, defensively.

"Whatever," she continued. "We're living there, and Carly and I come downstairs with our husbands prior to going out for dinner and a movie. No sooner do we walk into the room than Mom says, 'Just where do you all think you're going? There's a huge thunderstorm coming! I saw it on the Weather Channel a minute ago, so y'all are just going to have to stay in and watch TV with Daddy and me tonight.'"

"Yeah, and we won't be able to have company over during the week because we'll need our rest before we get up and go to work the next morning," Carly added.

"*Work*? She'll never let us *work*! That's for grown-ups. We'll be going to college 'til we're 65."

"Yeah, you're certainly right about that. And it'll be even worse after we have kids," Carly predicted. "She'll be telling us we're putting their diapers on upside down, or they're going to gouge their eyes out with their pacifiers."

"Yeah," laughed Chelsea. "Or they're gonna choke on their Cheerios. Remember that one?"

"Oh, my gosh, *yes!*" answered her sister, howling with laughter. "She had to cut ours into quarters before we could eat them."

"I wish!" said Chelsea. "That was what she did with our *grapes!* We never even got to *have* Cheerios!"

"You did, too, have Cheerios. You just had to let them get soggy in milk first," I corrected.

"Oh, and the *balloons!* We were the only kids who ever grew up suffering from Balloon Deprivation Syndrome. Our poor children would endure the same fate."

"Children *have* choked on balloons, I'll have you know," I exclaimed.

"And the fireworks! We couldn't even hold *sparklers*. 'Girls, don't get near those things! You'll catch your hair on fire! Look at what happened to Michael Jackson!'"

"What's even funnier is that I think she's serious about this commune thing."

"It's *not* a commune. It'll only be *our* family — all of us together — all the time! It'll be so much fun!" I happily informed them.

"No grapes, no Cheerios, no balloons. What fun," Carly groaned.

"I have a great idea. Let's go to China and get her some babies," suggested Chelsea.

"I have a *better* idea. Let's just go to China and *send* her some babies. She'd never find us there," countered Carly.

"Hmmmmm," I fantasized. "Chinese babies — little bitty, teeny baby girls. That's a *wonderful* idea! They'll love me, and let me dress them up in costumes for Halloween. And they'll sit on Santa's knee for me — *and* the Easter Bunny's. Of course, I'll have to baby-proof the house, and throw out all the grapes and Cheerios, and . . . ."

Cabin Boys and Squid Eyes

This past summer, I went deep-sea fishing. It was a bad decision — a very, very bad decision. The only reason I went was because my husband and our two daughters were going, and I knew I'd just sit around and worry about them all day and go completely neurotic if I didn't go with them, so I went.

It was a really pretty day — mostly clear skies, but very windy, with the accompanying rough sea.

The only experience I'd had with deep-sea fishing prior to this was about 30 years ago with my best friend and her dad aboard his fishing boat. We didn't venture out too far into the Gulf. As a matter of fact, the sweet dear took pity on me and stayed close enough to shore so that I could see land. I suppose that would actually be "shallow-sea" fishing.

Consequently, I was not at all prepared for the experience I was about to undergo on this excursion. In the first place, I thought it was just going to be us and maybe ten other passengers and the crew. How naïve can one person possibly be? I was also hoping that when my husband said, "65-foot boat," he actually meant 65-feet *wide*. He didn't. So there we were — more than 50 of us, plus the crew — on a 65-foot-*long* boat. With the four crew members, that made a total of, say, 55 people. Fifty-five people on a 65-foot boat. That comes out to about 1.18 feet per person. Not much room. Plus, *two hours* after we left the dock, and it was actually, *finally* time to fish, they lined us all up so close to each other against the rails that our elbows were nearly touching. From there, we had to "cast," if one can even call it that. We certainly couldn't throw our rods back behind us and cast far out without causing serious bodily injury to the people on the other side of the boat. And we had to bait our own hooks — with *squid*. Peee-ewww! Nasty, slimy, squid eyeballs staring back at you from your hook. Added to that, we had one-pound weights, or sinkers, or whatever they're called, hanging on the end of our line. One pound doesn't sound very heavy — until you've got one at the end of a fishing line. With all the squid-nibbling going on underwater, plus that weight, I spent all my time reeling in what I felt had to be at least a 100-pound marlin. Actually, all that I reeled in was the one-pound weight and the nearly microscopic bit of squid slime that remained on my hook.

After nearly four minutes of this exhausting exercise in futility, my *tailbone* was killing me, so I gave up my 1.18-feet of space and went inside the air-conditioned cabin. That was another disappointment. I had envisioned a handsome and strapping "cabin boy" serving mimosas to those of us who chose to retreat to the comfort of the chaise lounges, bar, or, at the very least, tub chairs and low tables in the boat's cabin. What I *got* were several grown men who should've taken motion sickness medication before they boarded, their heads hanging over five-gallon plastic pails, and making noises I could certainly have done without. And, just for the sake of variety, a crewmember was cutting up squid on the countertop. There were no mimosas, no chaise lounges, no bar, no tub chairs — and definitely *no cabin boys*. There were stark, utilitarian vinyl, backless seats against the sides of the cabin with wooden molding that hit me just at neck-level, so I couldn't even lean back. There were ice chests belonging to the passengers occupying nearly every square inch of the cabin floor, so there wasn't even any room for my feet.

After I'd had as much fun as I could stand in there, I gave up and went back on deck. The winds had picked up, so I had to basically grab for support as I lurched from the cabin to the rail where my family was fishing. I was grabbing ladders, ice chests, *legs*, anything that would keep me from busting my rear end or flying over the rails.

Most of the five-gallon pails that were provided to the fisherpeople for their catch were being used for other reasons (those stated above). What surprised me most was the fact that all but one pail was being used for that particular barfy reason by *men* (*and* boys, to be perfectly fair and honest). We women were surprisingly holding our own. I was proud. But having gone through weeks and weeks of morning sickness, this was wimp stuff to me.

After about 20 minutes of actual fishing (or, in my case, *watching* people fish), we turned around and headed back on the two-hour trip to the dock. (I never could understand why the fish couldn't swim a little bit closer to shore, nor was I provided an acceptable answer.) The wind was blowing like crazy as the boat literally *slammed* down into the water between the swells. I was holding on to my kids for dear life — *theirs* and mine. Our teeth are noticeably shorter now than they were when we left the dock.

Two hours out, two hours back, 20 minutes of fishing.

But the day wasn't a total loss. No marlin, sailfish, or even red snapper, but Les and the girls were able to catch some little fish that we were actually able to cook for dinner. They were really good — and quite a bargain — only $75 a pound.

The Amazing Shrinking Clothes

One of the very few things I've learned about doing laundry in all these years is that hot water tends to shrink clothes. No one bothered to tell me, though, that just plain old heat shrinks things, too. It's true. I have absolute proof. My husband just brought down all our fall and winter clothes from the attic. Nothing fits. My sweaters, skirts, and slacks have all shrunk. They're at least a full size smaller than they were when I packed them away in April. Maybe it's the humidity. It has to get near 100% up there, with no real ventilation or anything. Combine that with 100+° temperatures, and that's a surefire recipe for disaster. Strangest thing, is, though, that I didn't realize until today how much weight my husband and kids have lost since April. All their fall and winter clothes still fit. Weird, huh?

Was There Life Before Microwaves, Momma?

Momma, Chelsea asked me, "what was life like before microwaves and DVD players and cell phones?"

"Gosh, honey, that's a good question. Let me see if I can even remember." I responded, buying time. "Well, for one thing, before microwaves, we just heated leftovers either on the stove or in the oven."

"What about popcorn?" she questioned.

"Oh, popcorn. Well, we had what was called 'Jiffypop.' It came in a little disposable sort of frying pan thingy. We just put it on the stove and cooked it. It took a whole lot of shaking, though. That, I do remember. Oh, and it sort of ballooned up into what looked like an aluminum hot-air balloon."

"Weird," she said.

"Yeah, I guess, in retrospect, it was kinda weird. It tasted good, though."

"What about before VCR's and DVD players?" she queried.

"Well, actually, there *wasn't* anything before VCR's and DVD players. Whatever movies we saw, we saw at movie theaters — except, of course for the 8-millimeter stuff."

"Eight-millimeter?"

"Yeah, those were sort of along the line of eight-track tapes — Neanderthal technology, so to speak," I replied. "They were movies made that were displayed on projection screens. Rather crude, by today's standards."

"So, y'all couldn't go to, like, Blockbuster and rent movies?" she asked, pity perceptible in her voice.

"No, sweetie. There were no Blockbusters back then."

"So, definitely no DVD players?"

"Nope."

"Nintendo?"

"Unh-unh."

"Sony Playstation?"

"Nope."

"How could you *stand* it?" she asked, compassionately.

"Well, honey, it's like air-conditioning. If you never had it, you don't miss it." I responded. "Most of the technology you're experiencing now has come about in the past twenty years. Shoot, I remember having to wait five minutes for the TV to warm up before a picture actually appeared on the screen."

"You're *kidding*!" was her response.

"No, I'm not. And when we had parties, we had vinyl records that we could never depend on."

"What do you mean?"

"I mean that when we put something like 'In the Still of the Night' on the old hi-fi and started slow-dancing, we never new if we'd be able to actually finish the song without hearing 'In the st-st-st-st-st-ill . . . uh-uh-uh-uh-uhv . . . the ni-ni-ni-ni . . . .' because those old 45's were so easy to scratch. It could certainly ruin the mood."

"That's really sad," she sympathized.

"Yeah, but there's a whole lot of stuff that we had that was even better than what kids have today," I told her.

"Doesn't sound like it to me," she responded.

"Well, there was," I insisted.

"For instance?" she asked.

"Well, for instance, skates with keys, American Bandstand; angel hair on Christmas trees; the *real, original* Mickey Mouse Club; hula hoops; hopscotch; Roy Rogers and Dale Evans; '57 Chevys; Howdy Doody; 43¢ for a McDonald's hamburger, fries *and* a Coke; 25¢ for a gallon of gas. The list just goes on and on."

"But what about cell phones?" she asked me.

"The only 'cells' we knew about were those in jails or having to do with biology."

"Well, how did you keep in touch with each other?"

"By regular old phone," I responded.

"That's crazy."

"Yeah, I suppose you're right. But life was much easier back then," I informed her.

"If *you* say so," she responded, doubtfully.

I knew what she was saying, and I understood. But I also knew that there was nothing I could say that would convince her that life really was better "back then" — *all* movies were rated "G"; candy cost a penny; Cokes were a nickel; Mary Janes, penny loafers, and saddle shoes were all we needed — except for tennis shoes to wear with our dorky gym uniforms; our Moms were always there when we got home from school; and detergent boxes always contained "prizes" — towels, glasses, dishes. When we bought gas, we got our windshields washed, our oil checked and air put into our tires if they needed it — and we didn't even begin to know how to pump our own gas — that was always done for us. *And* we sometimes even got S&H Green Stamps, in addition to all that service.

I remember going steady and getting my boyfriend's class ring. I must have used five rolls of Scotch tape to make that ring fit. And he'd pick me up in his dad's '64 Ford, and I'd sit right next to him because it — and most other cars back then — didn't have bucket seats. And we'd go to drive-in movies every Friday night and park between other friends whose rituals were the same as ours. And we'd have to buy those little coils that we put on the dashboard and lit in a mostly futile effort to keep mosquitoes away. And in cold weather, we'd take blankets and snuggle and sometimes even watch the movies — always at least a double-feature, if not a triple.

"Well, what about computers?" she asked, bringing me back into the present.

"What about them, honey?"

"I mean, how did y'all get by without computers? How did you do school papers and that kind of stuff?"

"Well, we went to a building called a 'library' and consulted this archaic system libraries had of cataloging their books and other reference material — it was called a 'card catalog,' if I remember correctly. Then, we'd look all over the place for whatever books, magazines, periodicals or whatever we needed for our research. Then we'd gather all that information and bring it home and type it on a manual typewriter."

"What's that?" she asked.

"It was the precursor to the electric typewriter, which was the precursor to the word processor, which was the precursor to the computer. It was unbelievably prehistoric. You had to pretty much bang on the keys to type on it. And if we made mistakes, we had to erase them with this weird little wheel-looking thing with a brush on the end. And if we weren't very careful, we'd erase a hole in the paper and have to start all over again. We thought we'd died and gone to heaven when white-out was invented."

"Oh, Mom, that's really *sad*," she sympathized.

"That's okay, honey. In another forty years, your child will be saying the same thing to you. She'll be wondering how you got by without flying cars and robots to do your cooking. And she'll probably think you were crazy for having hair and wearing makeup and going on dates. She'll think football and dances were totally off the wall. Every generation finds the earlier ones outdated and ancient."

"Maybe you're right, Mom, but I just can't see things changing that much in forty years."

"Neither could I, honey. Neither could I."

Huh ?

Nothing — and no one else — on earth provides better fodder for my writing than my extended family. I've written about them time and time again. Having recently returned from an entire weekend family reunion in Alabama, I feel compelled to share some of the wit and wisdom I gleaned from my kinfolks in less than 48 hours — believe it . . . *or not.* This is exactly what is meant by the saying "truth is stranger than fiction."

First of all, the older folks feel compelled to pass along "sage" pieces of wisdom and advice — distorted though it may be. For example:

"Donkey see, donkey do."

"You can't judge a book by its contents."

"That's like the pot calling the kettle names."

"One bad apple don't make the pie taste no better."

"You can't teach an old woman new tricks."

"You can lead a duck to water, but you can't make him swim."

My personal favorite, though, is one uttered by Jackson, my cousin (very, very, *very* far removed, thank heaven). He came up with this lulu:

"An ounce of prevention is worth a can of Coors."

Confucius has no reason to worry.

Aint Weeder

I can recall how much fun was made of President Kennedy for saying "Cuber" instead of "Cuba." We all, regardless of — or perhaps *because of* — the geographical locations we reside in, talk a little funny. Case in point: I had a great-aunt whom I had always called "Aint Weeder" because everyone else called her that — or just plain "Weeder." For all the years I knew her, I thought it was a nickname she'd earned due to her incomparable gardening skills. It wasn't until I read her obituary that I learned that her real name was "Ouida" (pronounced "Weeda"). That same obituary also straightened me out about my Great-Aunt *"Wander."*

Will That Be Sweet or Unsweet, Hon?

As I write this chapter, I'm nearly at the end of my 20-city Southern book tour. It's been wonderful fun. I've visited some great cities and met some fabulous, fun, and charming people. I'm amazed, though, at how judgmental I've become — not about the people. What I've learned is that I'm a "tea snob."

The first "leg" of my tour took me to Texas — San Antonio, Houston, and Dallas, to be exact. It was sort of like "going home" again. Both of my daughters were born in Houston, and we lived there from 1981 until 1987.

I've always thought of Texas as more "Southwest" than "Southern" because of all the heavy "Western" influence there — cowboys, oil wells, and all. However, on February 2, 1861, they *did* secede from the Union, so . . . . But the true test came when I went to a San Antonio restaurant for lunch and ordered sweet tea.

"I'm sorry. We don't have *sweet* tea," my server informed me with what looked a little too much like a sneer.

Same thing happened in Houston and Dallas.

My next stop was Jacksonville, *Florida.*

No sweet tea there, either.

Then came Charleston, South Carolina.

"Will that be sweet or unsweet, hon?" the darlin'
waitress asked me. Music — *sweet, sweet music*— to my
ears.

I was raised on sweet (not "sweetened") tea. I had never
even tasted unsweetened (not "unsweet") tea until I met
my future husband's parents for the first time and had
dinner at their house. It took everything within me not to
make a dill pickle face when that tea hit my taste buds.

At my house, I make it really sweet. We call it
"Mamaw" tea, named after the way my sweet Mamaw
always made it — two cups of sugar to one gallon of tea.
Mmmmmmm. Pure glucose!

Charleston, Savannah, Atlanta and Nashville were all
there for me with sweet tea. Then I went to Orlando and
Tampa. The servers at the restaurants where I dined just
looked at me like I was possessed when I asked for that
delectable nectar.

I guess I might as well get prepared for vinegar on
pancakes at this rate — or *dill pickle pie.*

Grace Kelly, I Ain't

One of the real perks about being a published writer is sometimes getting to go on book tours. I'm almost at the end of my first one, as I finish this, my second book. This particular tour is what's referred to as a "driving tour," which, I guess, is pretty self-explanatory. Basically, what it means is that the driver's seat in my car is a lot *flatter* and the *actual driver's* "seat" (my rear end) is a lot *wider*. I've put thousands of miles on my car and the same number on my hiney.

I've eaten out in the past three months more than I have in the past three years, all totaled. *Thousands and thousands* of calories have been consumed on this tour, I must confess. A girl has to keep up her energy, doesn't she?

And, as always, I've been on the lookout for new material; and anyone who's ever read anything I've ever written knows that I have basically no shame. Consequently, I'm going to share with you one of my most humiliating experiences.

I was at a hotel in Orlando, Florida — far enough away from "that mouse place" to ensure myself of some peace and quiet (in other words, I was hoping for older children and "grownups"). And, as much as I do like *most* kids, I did find that I was mercifully blessed with a noticeable absence of the same at this particular hotel. So, there I was, drifting along on my inflated float in the hotel's beautiful pool early on the day of my signing. I was floating lazily on top of the beautiful aquamarine water. Much to my delight, since I was really craving solitude and relaxation, there were no other guests in the pool. As a matter of fact, the only people anywhere near the pool were all the young businessmen standing around outside the hotel's restaurant, adjacent to the pool, talking on their cell phones. Being a little overweight — okay, *more* than a little overweight, and a little older than they — okay, *more* than a little older, I knew they weren't paying any attention to me, anyway. They weren't paying any attention, that is, until the pool's enormous dolphin fountain, located directly in the center of the pool, unexpectedly sprang to life, spewing huge volcanic sprays of water from the mouths of the dolphins and knocking me totally off my float. I heard more stifled laughter and *"Oh, my gosh"*es than I'd ever want to hear again. Of course, several of them ran poolside to see if I was okay. I was fine, in spite of the fact that my hair looked like the Frankenstein monster's bride's because of the hairspray (I had intended *not* to get my hair wet, you see) and my eye makeup had liquefied into what looked like snail trails all down my face. And, try as I might — and, believe me, I *did* try — I could not remount my float.

"No, really, I'm fine," I reassured them as, again and again, my float pummeled me to the depths of the pool as I was repeatedly and simultaneously beaten down by the force of the merciless and unrelenting fountain. And, of course, the harder I tried to get back on my float, the less successful I was, all the while being beaten into oblivion by the unpitying, possessed fountain.

Finally, I gave up on the float and managed to make my way back to the side of the pool, attempting to salvage what was left of my dignity . . . and my *cranium*. I was sure I had black-and-blue marks covering my body. Thankfully, the young executives had tired of my "performance" and returned to their phone calls, so I was able to recover at least some semblance of my poise and pride — until I walked back into the hotel's lobby full of conventioneers and slid across its highly-waxed floor, landing on my . . . *driver's seat.*

I'm thinking my next book should be a how-to on grace and elegance. Who better to write that?

What the Heck is a Cleveland "Brown?"

I am counting down the days until college football season begins anew. And while I can't tell you when the first game takes place, or even who plays in it, I *can* tell you that my beloved Crimson Tide has its first game in 58 days from the date I'm writing this little ditty. Even though we're facing some tough times ahead because of sanctions and the doo-doo-heads in the NCAA, I predict The Tide will indeed *Roll!*

The University of Alabama's Crimson Tide became a part of my life around 1960 (that would make it ten years before I was even born — hmmmm, *strange*) when I first laid eyes on Joe Willie Namath. Actually, it was when I laid eyes on *his eyes*. Honey, at that moment, I knew it was over between me and Johnny Crawford ("Mark" on "The Rifleman"). Before that, I probably couldn't have even been able to tell you the difference between a football and a basketball; but after I saw Joe, all that changed. Knowing that the only way I could see him was to watch *The Tide* play football, I was at my nearby male cousins' house (they were the only ones who had a color TV) for every televised game (which their mother, my Aunt Joydeen, *made* them let me watch with them — and you can only imagine how popular that made me with them).

I had absolutely no idea what was transpiring on the field; and I probably couldn't have told you the difference between a goalpost and a referee. All I knew was that my future husband — he of the green eyes and big nose — was on that field. I held my breath every time he got tackled — or "downed" or whatever it was. I watched him every season, and followed him throughout his pro career, even though I'd since set my sights on Beatle Paul McCartney to be the father of my children.

I guess it's the same way with most football fans — particularly college and university fans. It just gets into one's blood and can turn that person into a true fanatic — thus the word "fan." Many fans paint their faces, and quite often their bodies, to demonstrate their devotion to their team; they scream, cheer, cuss or cry, and quite often do all of these things at the same time, depending on the circumstances.

Fans are easy to understand, though, if you're one of the more demonstrative types yourself. It's the mascot and/or nicknames that are a little more difficult for me to comprehend. The Crimson Tide was so named because an announcer (or someone) once said, many years ago, that they looked like a crimson tide running out onto the field (at least, that's the story I heard). So why, then, did they choose an elephant as a mascot? Granted, that particular elephant has gone from a somewhat non-menacing "Dumbo" type to the very intimidating, tusked, scowling one that now appears on Bama T-shirts, ball caps, and bumper stickers. Still, we have Alabama's Barney-like "Big Al" mascot prancing and dancing on the sidelines.

Not very threatening a'tall. And he's become the brunt of many snide remarks I've overheard when watching Bama games at public venues.

Then again, Alabama's not the only team that could've done better selecting a mascot. The Crimson Tide is a great name, at least. Many other teams don't even have that. There are, among others, the Oregon Ducks (ooooh, scary), the Oregon State Beavers, the Rice Owls (whooooo'd be afraid of them?), and the Texas Christian Horned Frogs (well, at least they're horned). What's next? Yakoma Yaks? Louisville Lambs? Denver Doves? Columbus Cockers? Chicago Chihuahuas? Pittsburgh Poodles? Palm Springs Pomeranians?

Teams need threatening, apocalyptic mascots — *predators*, for heaven's sake! How about the Vicksburg Vipers or the Anchorage Asps? And why not the Toledo Tasmanian Devils or the Waukeegan Warthogs or the Pittsburgh Pit Bulls? And there's always room for expansion teams like the Rochester Rottweilers, the Wichita Weimeraners and Schenectady Scorpions, not to mention the Tempe Tarantulas and Duluth Dobermans (Dober*men?*). Or how about some *real* predators — the Columbus Collection Agents or the Portland Personal Injury Attorneys — or, the very most terrifying of all, the Tallahassee . . . *Telemarketers?*

I'm an Oldie

Being a certified "oldie" (whatever in the world *that* means), one of my favorite television channels is TVLand. I absolutely love that channel. I can go back 30 or 40 years in two seconds — depending upon what show I'm watching at that moment. There's "Love Boat," which put "Cruise Director" at the top of my list of chosen careers. "Love Boat," with its fairy-tale happy endings and incredulous "plots" — if one can even call them that — a lecherous playboy doctor who never treated a sick passenger unless *she* was gorgeous, at least 20 years younger than he, and had an abundant "chestal" area; a captain who was never on the bridge; an insecure, homely purser whom love scorned time and time again; a bartender with no apparent psychology degree who was called upon to solve not only the passengers' love problems, but the crew's, as well. And then there was Julie — the Cruise Director — my idol, my hero — well, not really, because I was well into my twenties when "Love Boat" was airing; but she, out of all the crew members, seemed to have it, at least seemingly, "together."

There was always someone, usually only *one* person, on all of those 50's, 60's, and 70's shows who seemed to have it together. One of them was Opie on "The Andy Griffith Show." Andy chewed out poor little Opie on nearly every show, it seems, then ended up having to eat crow every single, doodah time because the child was just too sweet to do much harm.

And, of course, on "Father Knows Best," *Father* . . . knew best.

But the show that drove me the very most crazy was "Leave it to Beaver." Who, in his or her right mind, would leave *anything* to Beaver? The kid was, according to his cooler and *normal* older brother Wally, "a big goof." But, according to his parents, Beaver could do no wrong. Beaver could burn the original Declaration of Independence, wear the American flag as a diaper, and join the Communist Party; but, in June's and Ward's eyes, the little darlin' was their perfect baby boy. Wally, on the other hand, really was a decent kid — he made good grades, got what appeared to be a weekly haircut, never got into any serious trouble, and, unlike "The Beav," willingly took a daily bath.

Another thing I never understood about this particular show, besides the parents' blatant favoritism of Beaver, is why in the world anyone would even want to call their child "Beaver" — particularly in light of the fact that his last name was *Cleaver.* Granted, anyone named "Rebel" probably shouldn't be criticizing anyone else's name; but I doubt very seriously that my parents would have named me Rebel if my last name had been "Treble" or "Pebble."

And then there was "The Mary Tyler Moore Show." Mary Richards was an inspiration to those of us who were still single at 21 — or as my Great-Aunt Ivenia preferred to refer to that state of unmarried bliss, "manless." *Back in the day* (2002 *teenage-ese* for anything that happened more than two years ago), when I graduated from high school, it was common practice for a girl to be married within three months after graduation. As a matter of fact, I served as either maid of honor or bridesmaid in nine weddings in the summer of nineteen-aught-sixty-six, always making sure to stand way in the very back of the crazed mob of "teenaged spinsters" desperate to catch that bouquet of last chance. Married at 18 and pregnant at 19 was definitely *not* my idea of the perfect existence. No way. That's why I loved watching "The Mary Tyler Moore Show." Mary Richards had great hair, great clothes, a great job, and wonderful apartments. She dated interesting men, ate out a lot, and drove a Mustang. *What a life.*

Before the days of Mary was the decade of Westerns and doctors. I was torn, in my adolescence, between "Mark McCain" on "The Rifleman," and "Adam Cartwright" on "Bonanza" in my quest to be a cowboy's wife — and to be Mrs. Jim Kildare or Mrs. Ben Casey was the stuff of my pre-teen fantasies.

TV has changed a great deal since those innocent programs of chaste kisses and twin beds – and the latter was for *married* couples. There was absolutely *no* premarital sex (except, of course, on "The Love Boat" — although we never actually saw it happen). Heck, on "The Newlywed Game," the couples couldn't even say the word "sex." It was referred to as "whoopey."

At the risk of sounding too much like Archie Bunker — or like I'm 125 years old, those *were* the days — weren't they?

Yo! Liz!
Wanna Come Out and Play?

Hey, *may I speak with Liz, please?* I asked the man who answered the phone.

"I *beg* your pardon," answered the voice on the other end, a voice resonating with total disbelief and a large amount of pomposity.

"Is she in?"

"Is *whom* in, madam?" the snooty man asked.

"Well, how many people do you have living there named 'Liz,' for crying out loud?" This time, *I* was the one with disbelief in my voice.

"I can assure you we have *absolutely no one* named . . . '*Liz*' living here, madam," he responded icily.

"Well, then, what does Phil call her?"

"*Phil? Phil?* Madam, are you, *by any chance*, referring to the *Prince?*" he asked.

"Well, duh, yes. Liz's husband. You know, Chuck's and Annie's and Andy's and Eddie's daddy," I informed the poor doofus.

"*Chuck? Annie? Andy? Eddie?*" he screeched.

"Yes, surely you know *Chuck* — with the *ears* — the heir to the throne — Liz's firstborn baby boy. This *is* Buckingham Palace I've reached, is it not?" I asked the apparently uninformed butler or whatever he was.

"Yes, madam, it is, but . . . ."

"Then, will you *please* put Liz on the phone. This *is* long-distance, you know, and I didn't call collect," I admonished, my patience with this poor man wearing thin.

"It's all right, Sinclair. I have it," spoke the familiar voice on yet another palace line.

"*Liz? Liz? Is that really you?*" I asked hopefully.

"This is Elizabeth II, *Queen of England.* And *you* would be?" she inquired, somewhat snobbishly.

"Well, finally! You know, you and Phil and the kids need to spend a little more time with ol' Sinclair. He doesn't have a clue what's going on in that house, let alone who even *lives* there," I advised her.

"May I ask the nature of your call, madam? And, once again, who *are* you?" Liz asked.

"Oh, I'm sorry! How rude of me. Well, my name is Rebel Lowrey Covan, and I'm calling from beautiful Pensacola, Florida, home of sugar-white sand; the incomparable Blue Angels; Roy Jones, Jr.; Don Sutton; . . . ."

"Yes, yes, yes. I understand that part, but *why* are you calling me? And how on earth did you get my private phone number?" she asked incredulously.

"Oh, I got your number from Sarah — you know, one of your ex-daughters-in-law. We attended several Weight Watchers meetings together. She's one wild woman, Liz! I'd keep my eye on that one, if I were you! Quite the party girl! Oh, and the reason I'm calling is that I've recently started a local chapter of the Red Hat Society — you know, the women who band together to celebrate growing old any way but gracefully. We pledge to sit on the sidewalk and learn how to spit, and all that. Anyhoo, our group is called The Tallulah Belles — we're named after Tallulah Bankhead. Speaking of 'party girls,' she'd have even given ol' Sarah a run for her money. Well, we are a fun bunch of women, ranging in age from 40 to — well, heck, some of our ladies are even older than *you*, Liz! You'd just love us! Well, I'm calling to see if you could be our guest speaker in, say, April or May. I thought maybe you could show us how to conduct a 'real' High Tea — the kind y'all have over there — you know, with the scones and crumpets and all. I figured if anyone could do that, it would be you, Liz."

"I *beg* your pardon!" she exclaimed.

"Boy, you and Sinclair certainly have that pardon-begging down pat! Oh, before I forget, since you're *well* over 50, you're going to have to wear a purple outfit and red hat. I'm thinking something kind of dressy for the tea; but you can just wear sweats, or maybe jeans and a casual purple sweater for our fun event. The hat part shouldn't be a problem for you, I wouldn't think, since I've never even seen you without a hat. Do you *sleep* in those things, Liz? Just kidding! But seriously, with the hats, please try extra hard to find something kind of funky. No offense, Liz, but those things you wear are just way too frumpy. They don't do anything for you. I'd suggest maybe just getting a straw cowgirl hat and you can just spray-paint it red — a lot of the girls do that. It'll save you a buck or two, honey. Then you can get some big purple grapes and just hot-glue those on there. Would that be cute — *or what!* Phil would have a hard time keeping his hands off you once he saw you in that hat!

"So, Liz, what do you think? April or May? I'd strongly suggest April because we're getting a busload of girls together to go over to Biloxi to see 'The Elvis Show' at one of the casinos. It's going to be *so* much fun! Just be sure to bring several pairs of purple panties to throw onto the stage. You can get some great ones at Frederick's of Hollywood. They've got them with feathers and sequins and all," I advised her, as I heard a familiar buzzing tone on the other end of the line.

"Hello? Hello? Liz? Hello?"

How rude!